# Breathing

## How we use air

# Contributors

Author: **Jinny Johnson BA FZSL** is a writer and editor of books for children and adults on natural history and science. She is also the author of *Skeleton: Our body's framework* in this series.

Series consultant: **Richard Walker BSc PhD PGCE** taught biology, science, and health education for several years before becoming a full-time writer. He is a foremost author and consultant specializing in books for adults and children on human biology, health, and natural history. He is the author of *Heart: How the blood gets around the body, Making Life: How we reproduce and grow, Muscles: How we move and exercise,* and *Brain: Our body's nerve center* in this series.

## Advisory panel

*1 Heart: How the blood gets around the body*
**P. M. Schofield MD FRCP FICA FACC FESC** is Consultant Cardiologist at Papworth Hospital, Cambridge, UK

*2 Skeleton: Our body's framework*
**R. N. Villar MS FRCS** is Consultant Orthopedic Surgeon at Cambridge BUPA Lea Hospital and Addenbrooke's Hospital, Cambridge, UK

*3 Digesting: How we fuel the body*
**J. O. Hunter FRCP** is Director of the Gastroenterology Research Unit, Addenbrooke's Hospital, Cambridge, UK

*4 Making Life: How we reproduce and grow*
**Jane MacDougall MD MRCOG** is Consultant Obstetrician and Gynecologist at the Rosie Maternity Hospital, Addenbrooke's NHS Trust, Cambridge, UK

*5 Breathing: How we use air*
**Mark Slade MA MBBS MRCP** is Senior Registrar, Department of Respiratory Medicine, Addenbrooke's Hospital, Cambridge, UK

*6 Senses: How we connect with the world*
**Peter Garrard MA MRCP** is Medical Research Council Fellow and Honorary Specialist Registrar, Neurology Department, Addenbrooke's Hospital, Cambridge, UK

*7 Muscles: How we move and exercise*
**Jumbo Jenner MD FRCP** is Consultant, and **R. T. Kavanagh MD MRCP** is Senior Registrar, Department of Rheumatology, Addenbrooke's Hospital, Cambridge, UK

*8 Brain: Our body's nerve center*
**Peter Garrard MA MRCP** is Medical Research Council Fellow and Honorary Specialist Registrar, Neurology Department, Addenbrooke's Hospital, Cambridge, UK

# Breathing

## How we use air

Jinny Johnson

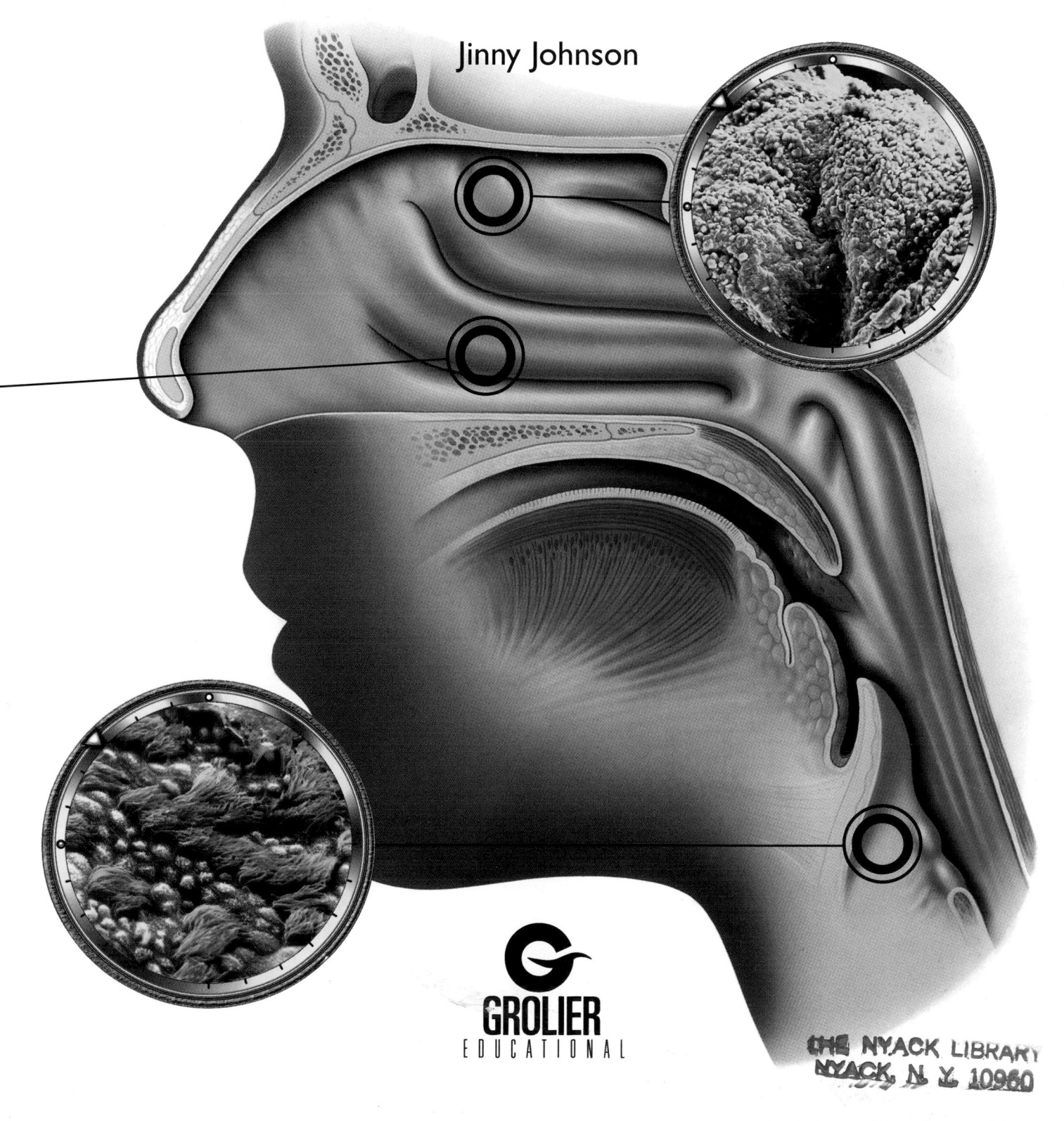

GROLIER
EDUCATIONAL

# ABOUT THIS BOOK

First published in 1998 by
Grolier Educational
Sherman Turnpike
Danbury
Connecticut

Set ISBN 0-7172-9265-7
Volume ISBN 0-7172-9273-8

Library of Congress Cataloging-in-Publication Data

Under the microscope : the human body
      p.      cm.
   Includes bibliographical references and index
   Contents: v. 1. Skeleton - v. 2. Brain - v. 3. Heart - v. 4. Making life - v. 5. Senses - v. 6. Digesting - v. 7. Muscles - v. 8. Breathing.
   ISBN 0-7172-9265-7 (set)
   1. Human physiology - Juvenile literature. 2. Human anatomy - Juvenile literature. 3. Body, Human - Juvenile literature.
[1. Human physiology. 2. Human anatomy. 3. Body, Human.]
I. Grolier Educational (Firm)
QP37,U53  1998
612–DC21
97-38977
CIP
AC

Produced by Franklin Watts
96 Leonard Street
London EC2A 4RH

Creative development by
Miles Kelly Publishing
Unit 11
The Bardfield Centre
Great Bardfield
Essex CM7 4SL

Printed in Belgium

Designed by Full Steam Ahead

Illustrated by Michael Courtney

Artwork commissioning Branka Surla

**Under the Microscope** uses microphotography to allow you to see right inside the human body.

The camera acts as a microscope, looking at unseen parts of the body and zooming in on the body's cells at work. Some microphotographs are magnified hundreds of times, others thousands of times. They have been dramatically colored to bring details into crisp focus and are linked to clear and accurate illustrations that fit them in context inside the body.

New words are explained the first time that they are used and can also be checked in the glossary at the back of the book, which includes a helpful pronunciation guide.

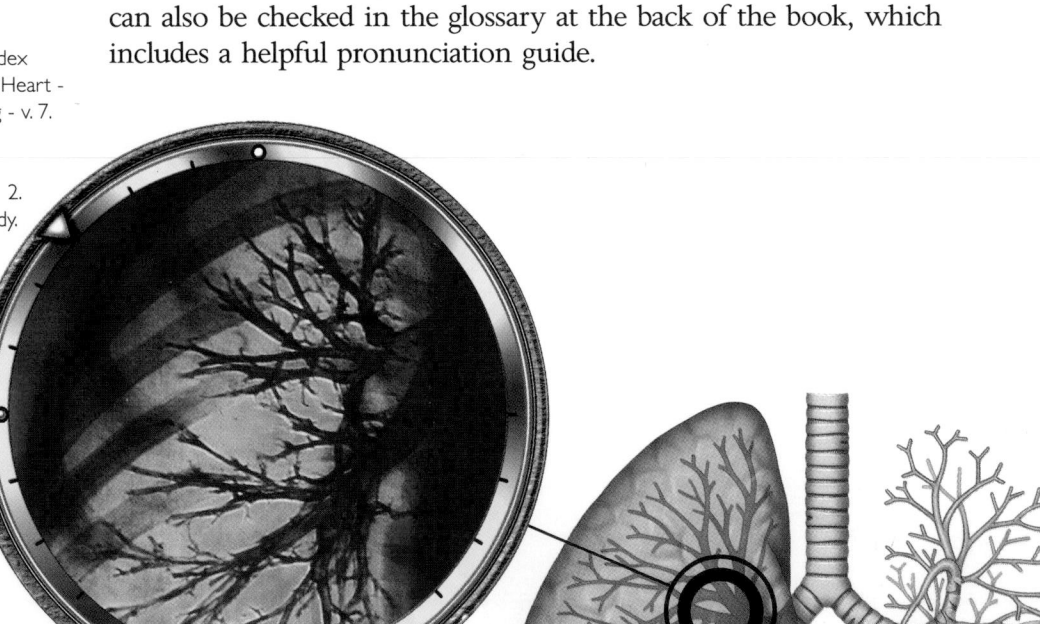

**Branching pathways**
A look inside the lungs (right) shows the branching airways that carry air in and out. The special X-ray (above) reveals the mass of branching blood vessels that transport blood into the lungs to pick up oxygen.

# CONTENTS

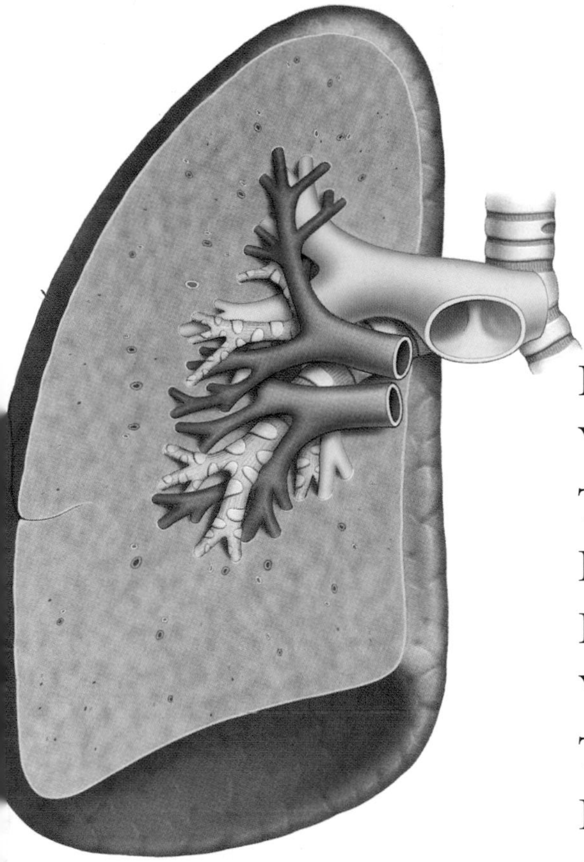

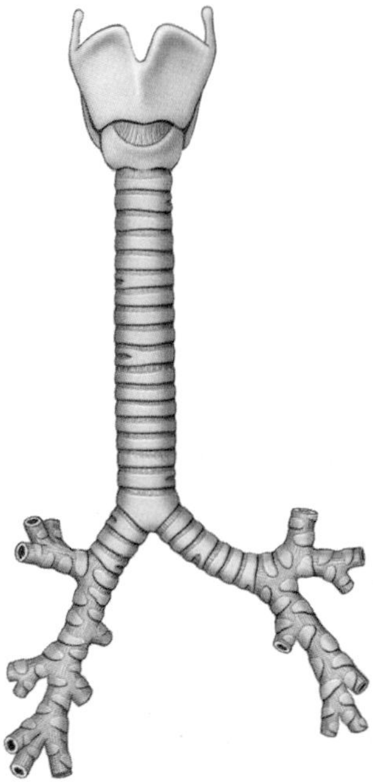

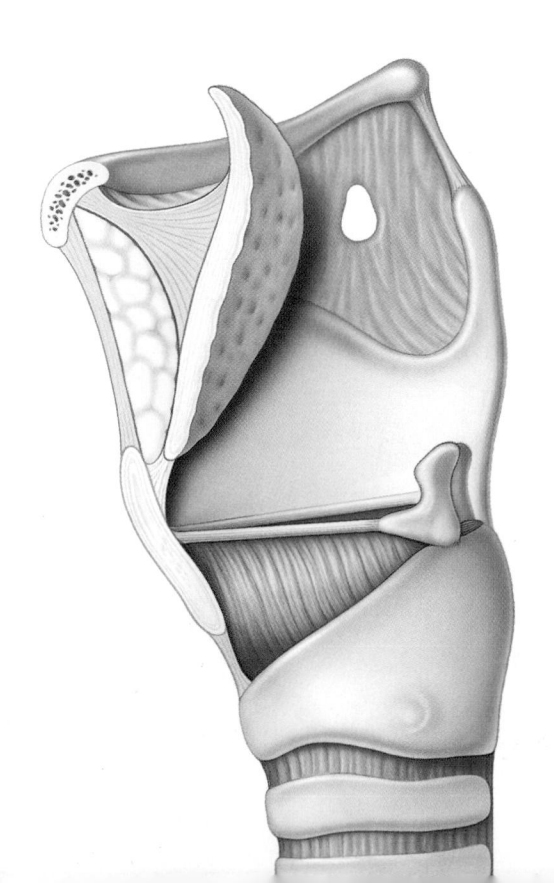

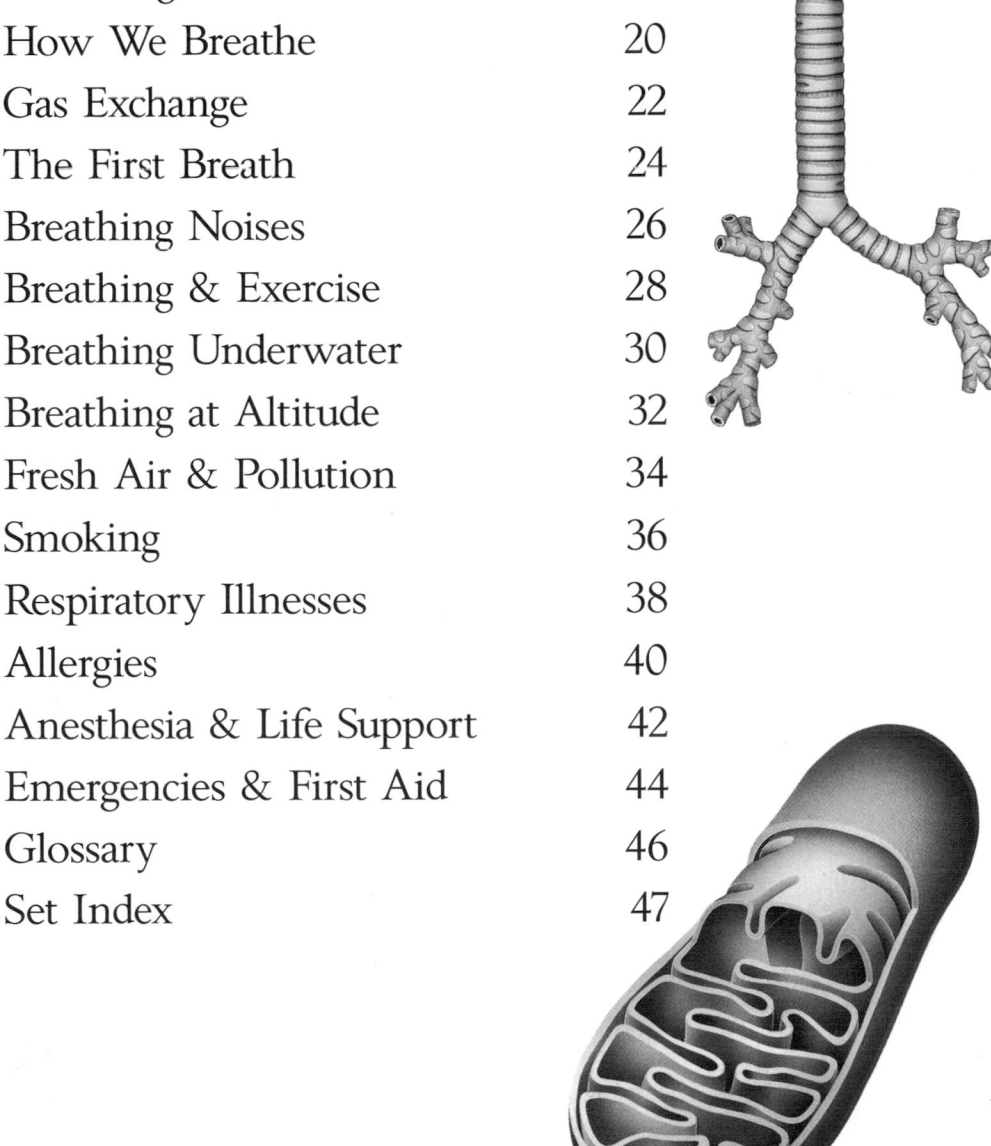

# INTRODUCTION

The first thing you do if someone has an accident is to check that he or she is breathing. Breathing air, like taking in water and food, is essential for life. Without the oxygen contained in air we cannot survive more than a few minutes.

Breathing happens automatically about 12 times a minute – we do not have to think about it. In an average lifespan of about 70 years a person takes at least 600 million breaths.

Oxygen fuels the processes of our bodies. But for the first three billion years of Earth's history there was no oxygen. The simple life forms that existed did so without oxygen. Then about one and a half billion years ago things began to change. More complex organisms evolved, including blue-green algae, familiar today as the green slime on the surface of ponds.

The algae used water and carbon dioxide in the process of photosynthesis and gave off oxygen as a waste product. Experts believe that this transformed the Earth's atmosphere, and now almost all creatures, including humans, depend on oxygen for life.

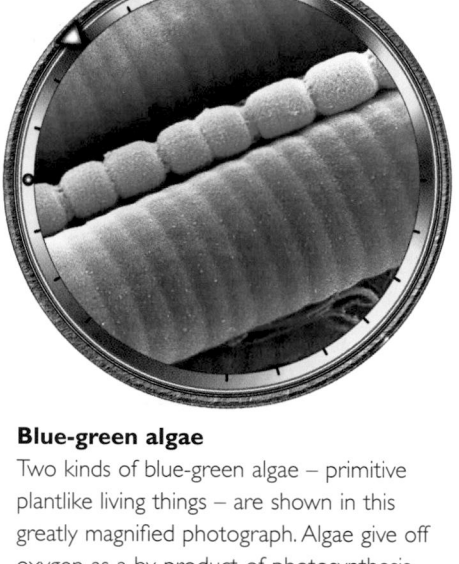

**Blue-green algae**
Two kinds of blue-green algae – primitive plantlike living things – are shown in this greatly magnified photograph. Algae give off oxygen as a by-product of photosynthesis.

**Keeping the airways clear**
The tiny hairlike cilia that line the windpipe, or trachea, are shown in the micrograph, below left. The cilia beat to move mucus and other debris along, keeping the airways free. Magnified cilia are also shown in the micrograph, right.

**Breathing out**
A special technique known as Schlieren photography shows the air disturbance caused by a person breathing out through the mouth.

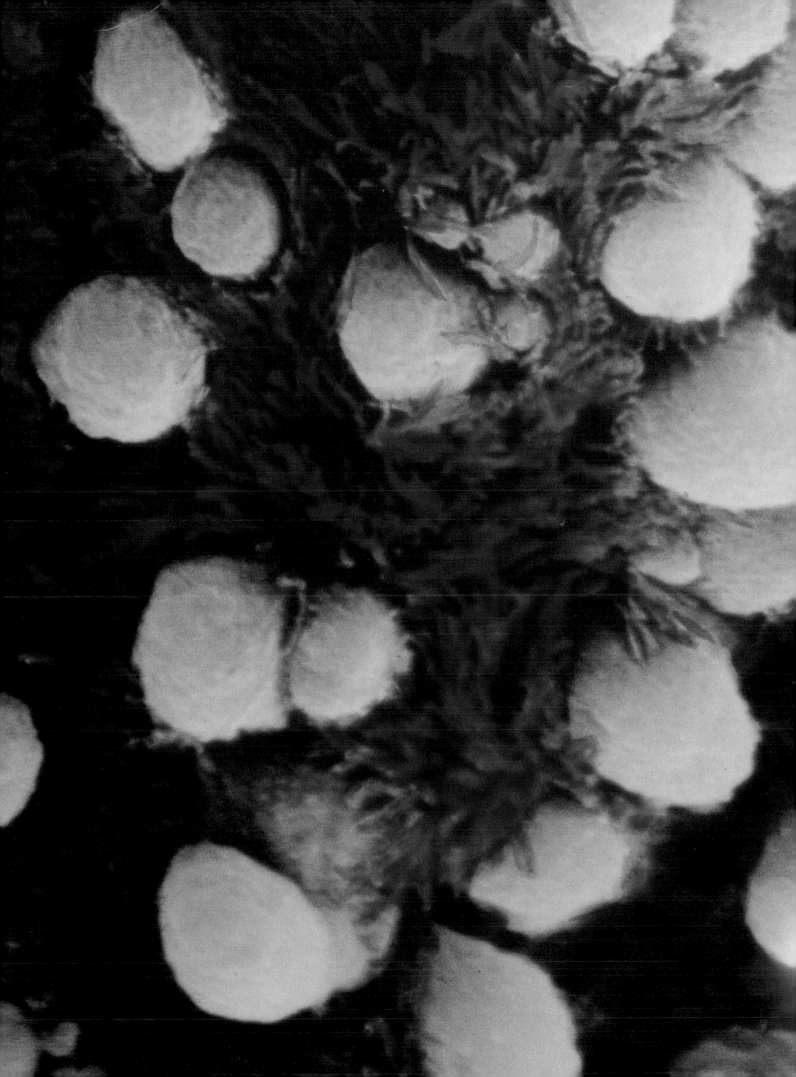

# WHY WE BREATHE

We breathe in order to take oxygen into our bodies and get rid of carbon dioxide. But the oxygen does not stop at the lungs. It is carried in the blood to all the body's cells, where the invisible work of respiration takes place.

The body's cells need oxygen in order to grow, to break down nutrients, and supply the body with energy. This constant activity is called metabolism. Without oxygen the cells cannot do their job and they die. A product of the cell's metabolism is carbon dioxide, and this is removed from the body when we breathe out. If carbon dioxide is not taken away from the cells, they cannot go on functioning. The carbon dioxide passes from the cells into the blood and is carried back to the lungs and breathed out.

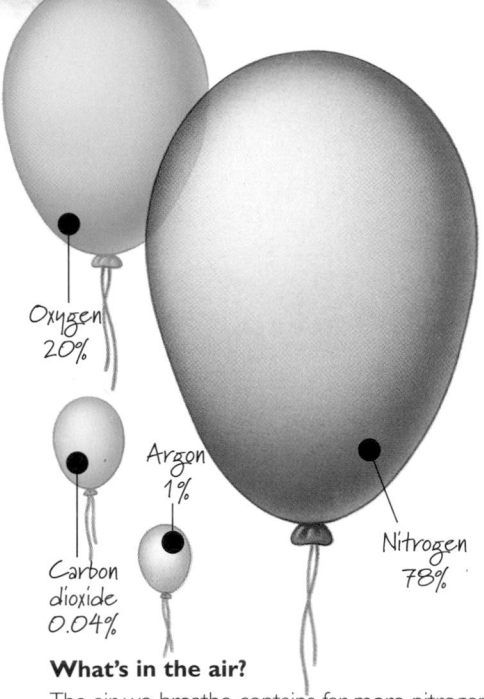

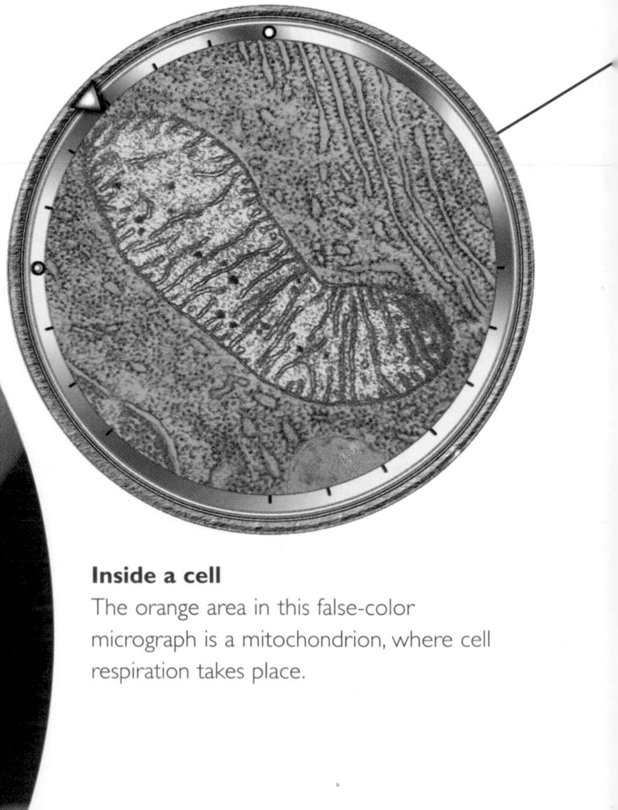

Oxygen 20%

Argon 1%

Carbon dioxide 0.04%

Nitrogen 78%

**What's in the air?**
The air we breathe contains far more nitrogen than oxygen. It also contains some carbon dioxide and small amounts of other gases, including argon, as well as water vapor.

**Inside a cell**
The orange area in this false-color micrograph is a mitochondrion, where cell respiration takes place.

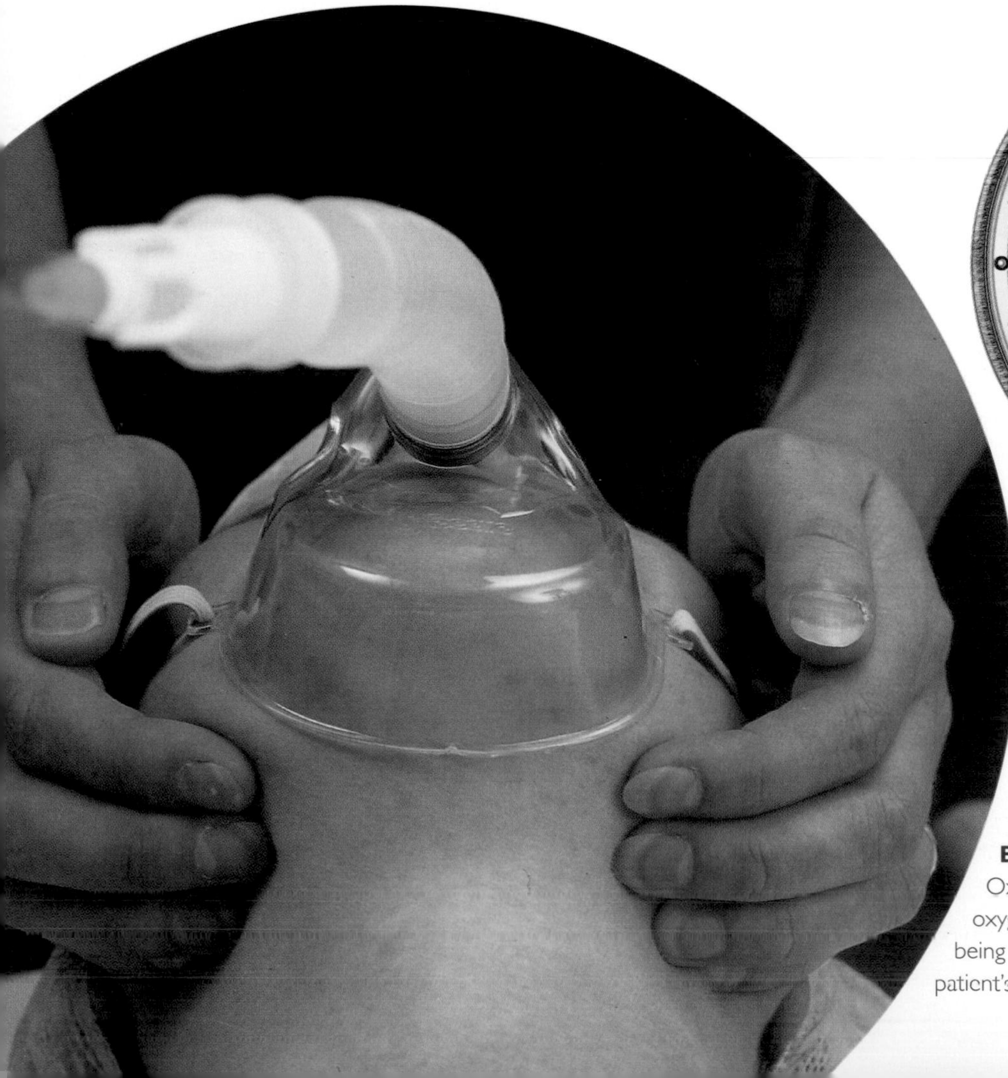

**Breathing help**
Oxygen is essential for life. This person is being given oxygen through a mask to help him recover after being anesthetized for surgery. The nurse is holding the patient's chin up to keep the airways as open as possible.

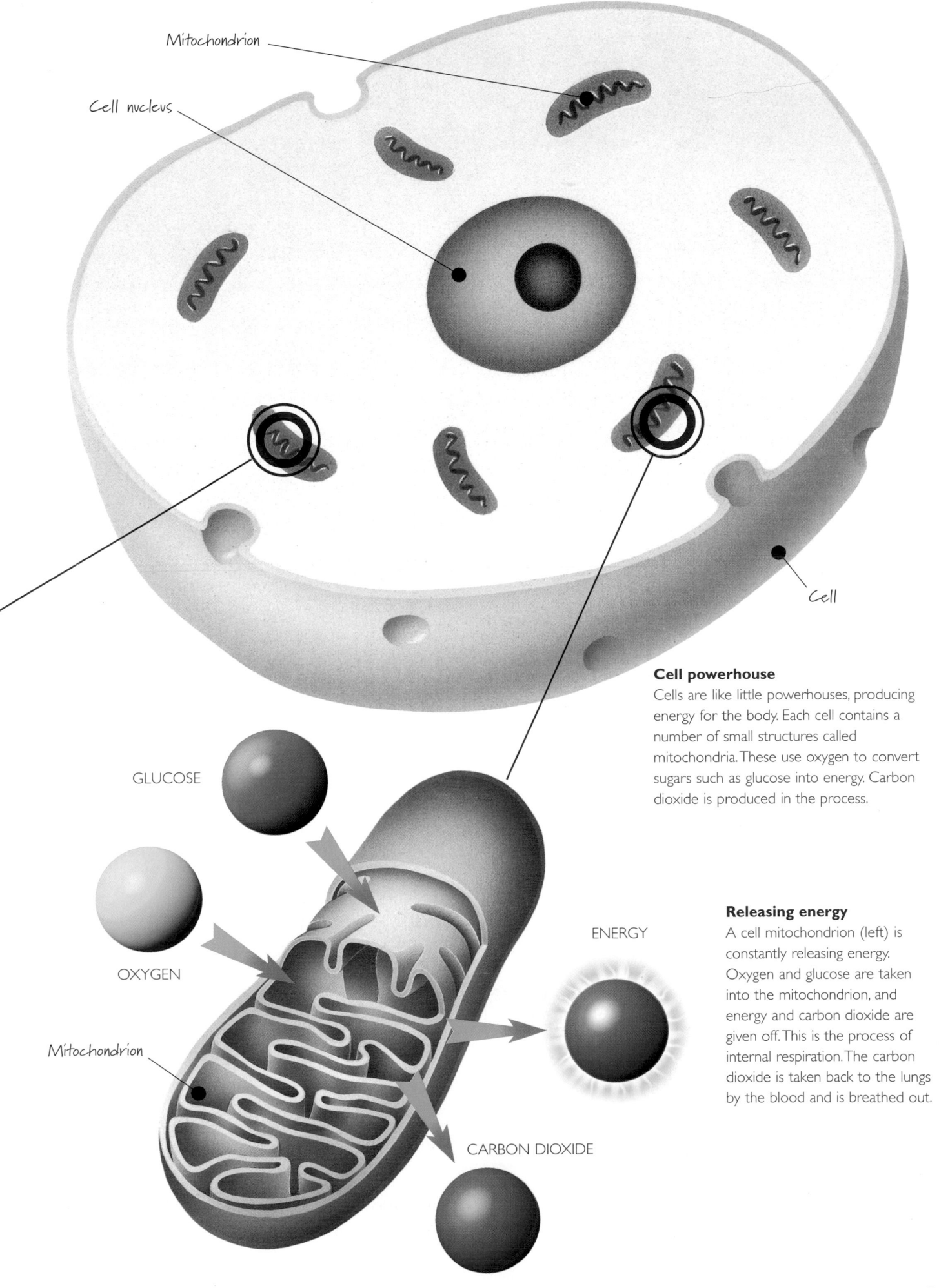

Mitochondrion

Cell nucleus

Cell

GLUCOSE

OXYGEN

Mitochondrion

ENERGY

CARBON DIOXIDE

## Cell powerhouse
Cells are like little powerhouses, producing energy for the body. Each cell contains a number of small structures called mitochondria. These use oxygen to convert sugars such as glucose into energy. Carbon dioxide is produced in the process.

## Releasing energy
A cell mitochondrion (left) is constantly releasing energy. Oxygen and glucose are taken into the mitochondrion, and energy and carbon dioxide are given off. This is the process of internal respiration. The carbon dioxide is taken back to the lungs by the blood and is breathed out.

# THE BREATHING ORGANS

The respiratory system of a human being is made up of several different parts. Most important of these are the nose, throat, voice box, windpipe, air tubes, and lungs.

Air generally enters through the nose and passes through the throat – called the pharynx – and the voice box into the windpipe. From here it passes into the air tubes, called bronchi, one of which passes into each lung. These branch into smaller and smaller tubes – the bronchioles. The bronchioles end in tiny air sacs called alveoli.

Oxygen passes through the thin walls of the alveoli and into the blood, where it combines with hemoglobin, the red substance in red blood cells. At the same time, carbon dioxide passes out of the blood into the alveoli, so that it may be breathed out.

Also involved in the process of breathing are the ribs, chest muscles, and diaphragm. The diaphragm is a sheet of muscle that divides the chest from the abdomen. This moves downward to make the chest cavity bigger when we breathe in. At the same time, the chest muscles contract to pull the ribs up, which also increases the size of the chest cavity.

**An automatic process**

We breathe all the time, even when we are asleep. The body automatically keeps a check on the amount of oxygen and carbon dioxide in the blood. If there is not enough oxygen or too much carbon dioxide, breathing speeds up to obtain more oxygen and get rid of excess carbon dioxide. When the balance is right, breathing slows again.

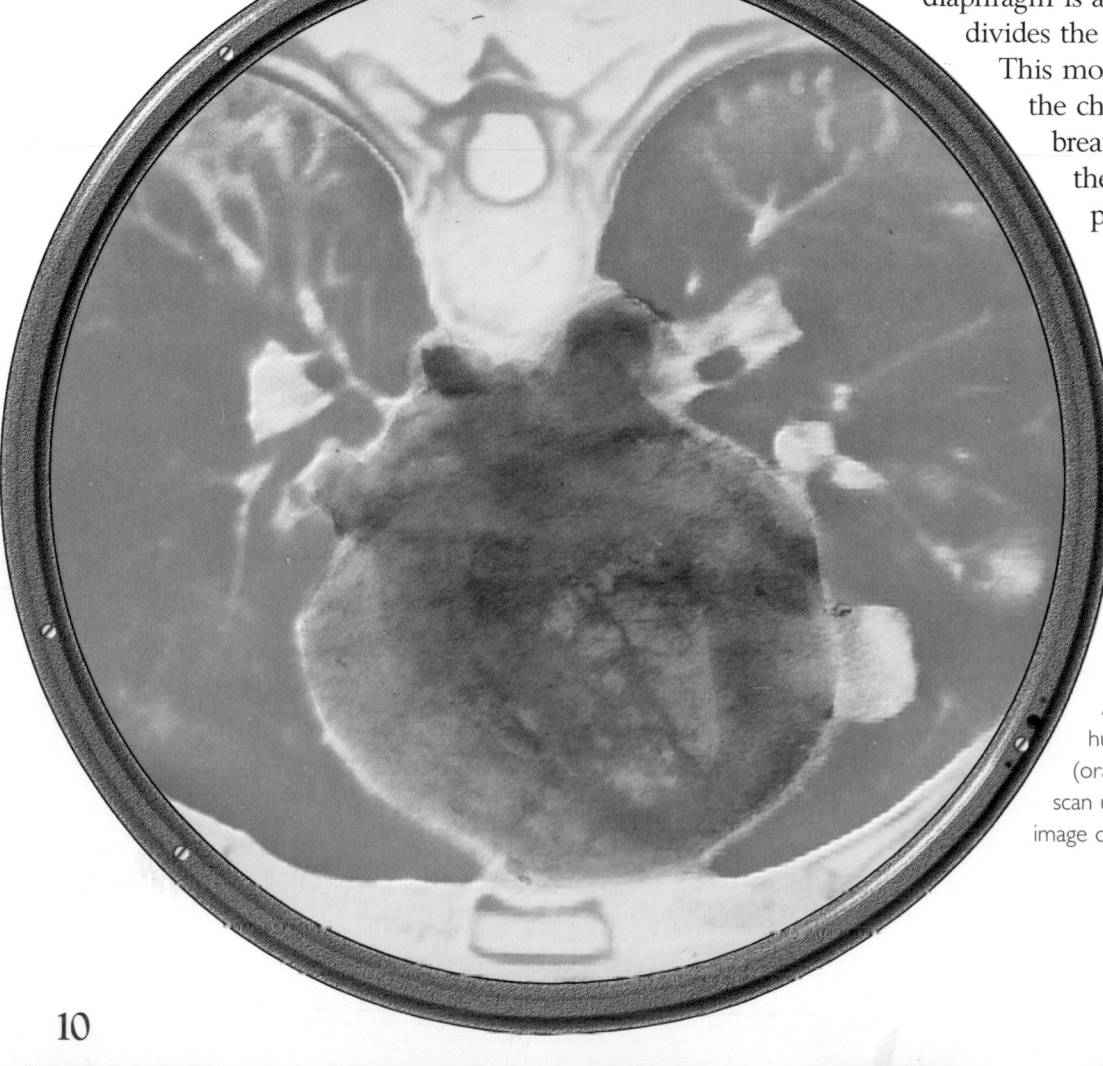

**A scan of the lungs**

A special CT scan through the human chest shows the heart (orange) and the lungs (blue). A CT scan uses fine X-ray beams to take an image of a slice through the body.

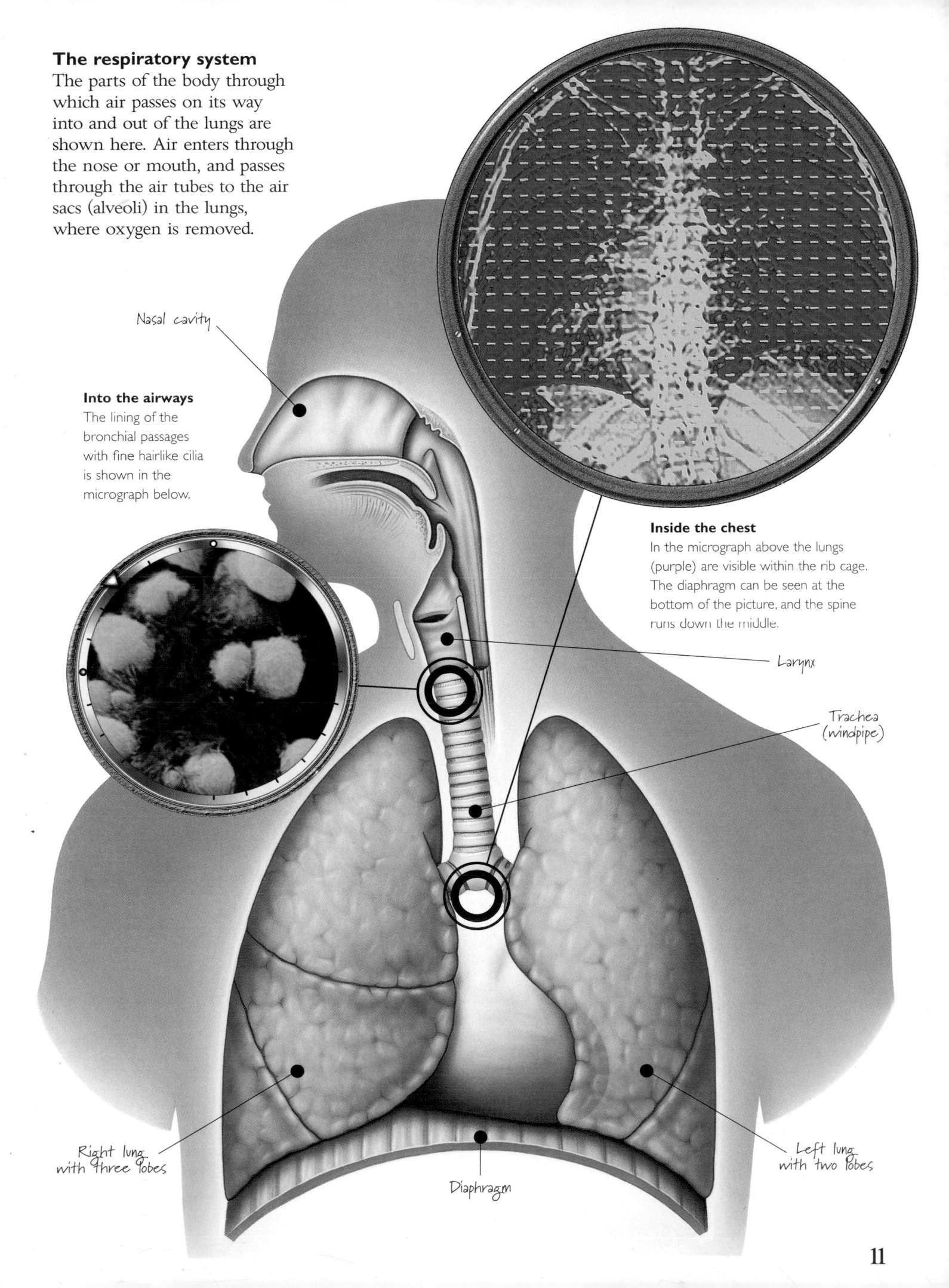

## The respiratory system

The parts of the body through which air passes on its way into and out of the lungs are shown here. Air enters through the nose or mouth, and passes through the air tubes to the air sacs (alveoli) in the lungs, where oxygen is removed.

Nasal cavity

### Into the airways

The lining of the bronchial passages with fine hairlike cilia is shown in the micrograph below.

### Inside the chest

In the micrograph above the lungs (purple) are visible within the rib cage. The diaphragm can be seen at the bottom of the picture, and the spine runs down the middle.

Larynx

Trachea (windpipe)

Right lung with three lobes

Left lung with two lobes

Diaphragm

# NOSE & THROAT

You can breathe in through your nose or mouth. It is useful to be able to breathe through your mouth, especially when you need extra oxygen after exercise, but it is generally better to breathe through your nose. This is because special structures in the nose warm and clean the air before it passes further into the body.

When air enters the nostrils, it passes into a cavity behind the nose that is lined with a mucous membrane. The sticky mucus produced by this membrane helps catch any dust or other particles so they do not reach the lungs. Tiny hairs called cilia on the membrane drive the mucus and dust down to the throat, or pharynx, where they can be swallowed. The air is also warmed in this cavity. The clean, warm air then passes into the upper part of the pharynx on its way to the lungs.

At the top of the nasal cavity are special nerves called olfactory nerves that allow us to sense smells carried in the air. Notice that when you want to smell something better, you sniff. This carries more air up to the nerve endings at the top of the nasal cavity and so helps you to detect the smell.

**Dust filter**

Lining the nose is tissue called epithelium. This makes mucus, which helps trap dust and other particles and stop them reaching the lungs. The epithelium can be seen at the top of this micrograph.

**The cilia**

A dense carpet of cilia lines the passages in the nose. The cilia beat constantly to and fro to move any dirt or foreign bodies out of the respiratory system.

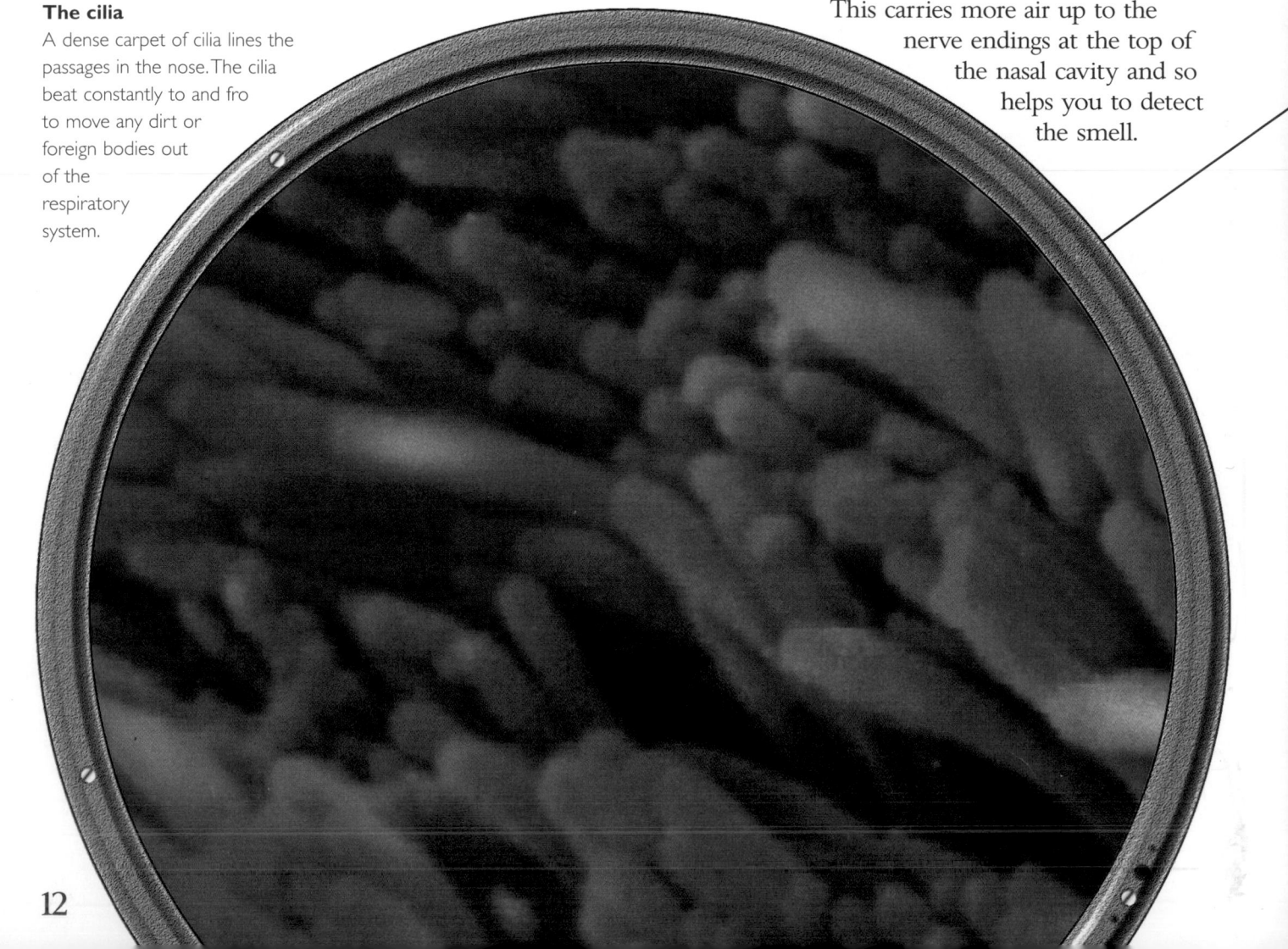

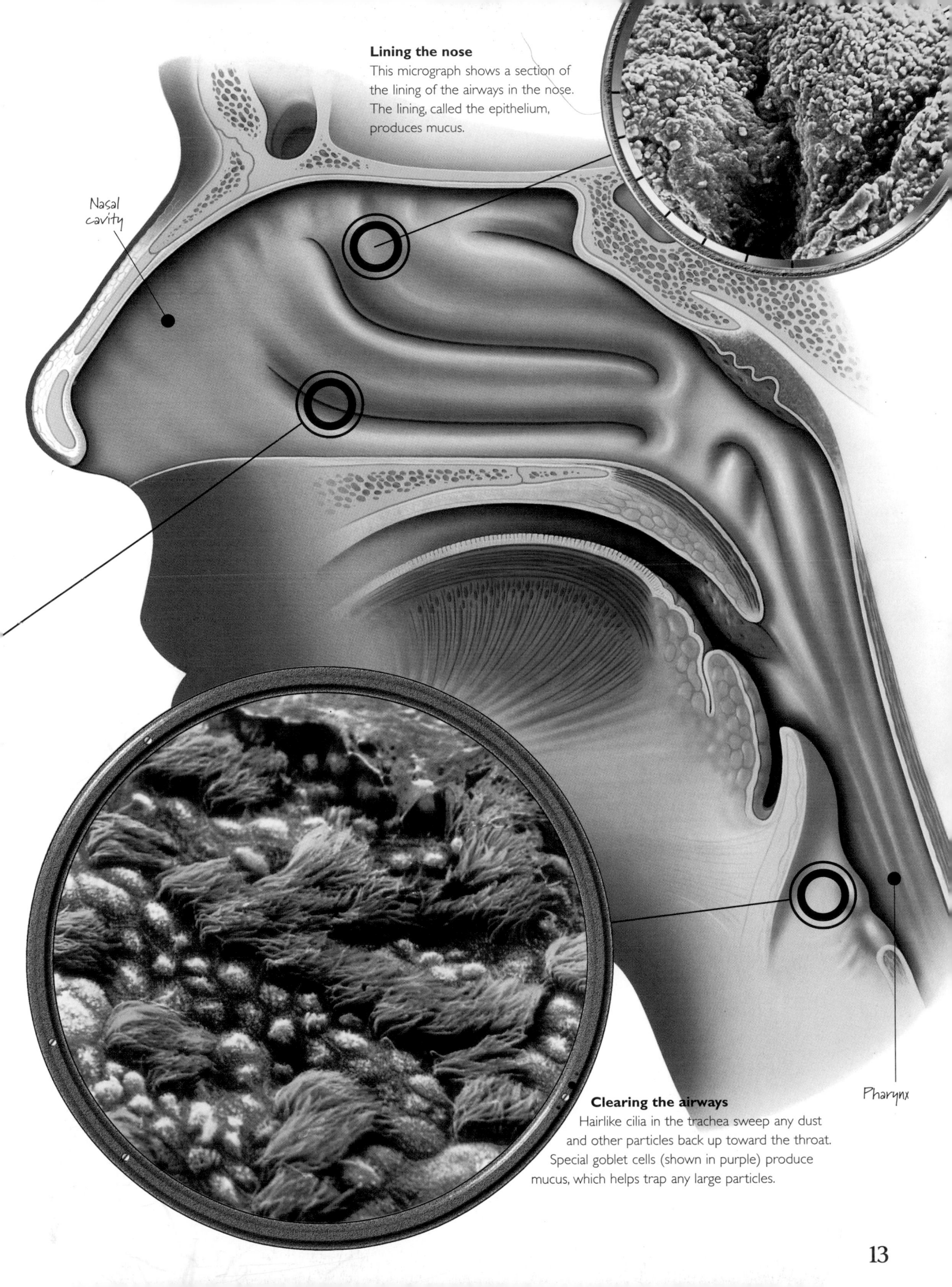

**Lining the nose**
This micrograph shows a section of the lining of the airways in the nose. The lining, called the epithelium, produces mucus.

Nasal cavity

Pharynx

**Clearing the airways**
Hairlike cilia in the trachea sweep any dust and other particles back up toward the throat. Special goblet cells (shown in purple) produce mucus, which helps trap any large particles.

# How We Speak

The voice box, called the larynx, lies below the pharynx. Air passes through it on its way to the lungs. Above the larynx is a small flap of tissue called the epiglottis, which covers it when we swallow food or drink. This stops food from going down the wrong way – into the air tube instead of the gullet or esophagus.

The outer part of the larynx is made up of cartilage – a tough, flexible material.

Inside the larynx are two folds of membrane called the vocal cords. When we are breathing normally, there is a wide gap between the cords through which air passes. But when we speak, muscles pull on the cords to close the gap between them. As air squeezes through the narrow gap, the cords vibrate, making sounds. We use our lips and tongue to shape the sounds into speech. The tighter the cords, the higher the sound made by the voice.

**The voice box**
The larynx, containing the vocal cords, lies in the throat at the top of the trachea.

**Open vocal cords**
The vocal cords lie open during normal breathing (left).

Epiglottis

**Adam's apple**
The largest piece of cartilage in the larynx is called the thyroid cartilage. Men have a large thyroid cartilage that makes a bulge at the front of the neck called the Adam's apple.

Vocal cords

**Contracted vocal cords**
For speech the vocal cords are pulled tight, making a narrow gap through which air is forced. This produces sound.

Rings of cartilage

14

## Speaking out

The larynx makes a sound as air passes through the vocal cords inside it. But to produce language, these sounds must be made into words by movements of the tongue, lips, roof of the mouth, teeth, and jaws.

### The "o" sound
The lips form an "o" shape to make the "o" sound.

### The "l" sound
In forming the "l" sound the tongue is placed against the back of the top front teeth.

### The "t" sound
For the "t" sound the tongue is placed firmly against the roof of the mouth for a second.

### In full song
Singing, like speech, is produced by the vibrations of the vocal cords. The sound resonates in the mouth and chest. Trained singers are able to control their breathing in order to pace their song correctly.

15

# WINDPIPE & BRONCHIAL TREE

The windpipe, or trachea, joins the upper part of the respiratory system to the lungs. In an adult the trachea is about 4 inches (11 centimeters) long and 1 inch (2 centimeters) across.

It is supported by about 20 horseshoe-shaped rings of cartilage. If you gently touch the front of your throat, you can feel these rings of cartilage. At the back of the trachea there is a muscle layer that can pull the rings of cartilage together if any foreign body does enter the tube. This stops it passing any further into the airways.

The bottom of the windpipe splits into two branches, called bronchi. One enters the right lung and the other the left lung. In the lungs the bronchi branch again to form tubes leading to the lobes of each lung. Within each lung the bronchi divide into smaller and smaller tubes, making a system that looks like an upside-down tree. The smallest of these tubes are called bronchioles.

**A bronchial tree**

The bronchial tree of the human respiratory system has been modeled, using the airways as a mold. Here the main bronchi are colored orange.

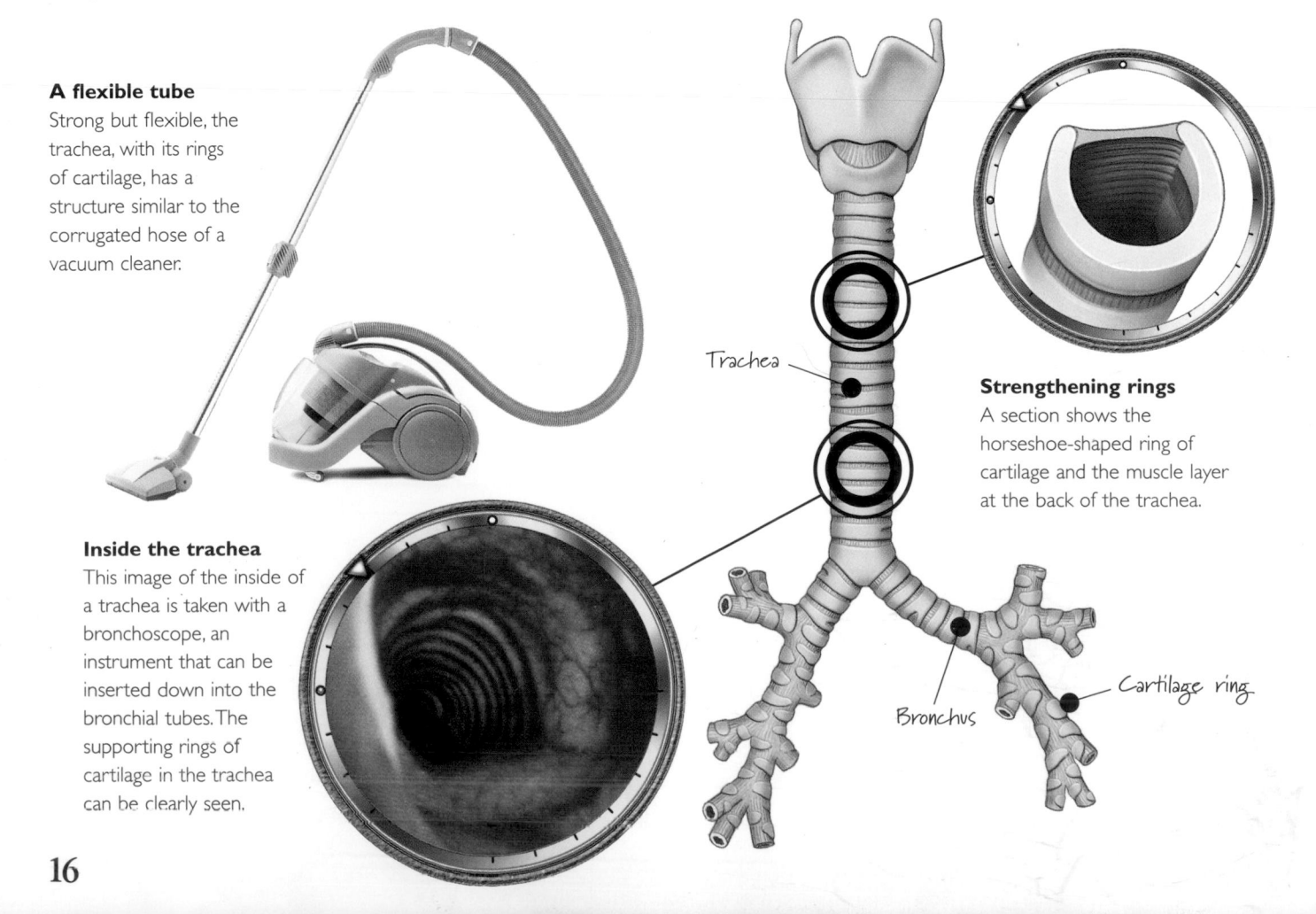

**A flexible tube**
Strong but flexible, the trachea, with its rings of cartilage, has a structure similar to the corrugated hose of a vacuum cleaner.

**Inside the trachea**
This image of the inside of a trachea is taken with a bronchoscope, an instrument that can be inserted down into the bronchial tubes. The supporting rings of cartilage in the trachea can be clearly seen.

Trachea

**Strengthening rings**
A section shows the horseshoe-shaped ring of cartilage and the muscle layer at the back of the trachea.

Bronchus

Cartilage ring

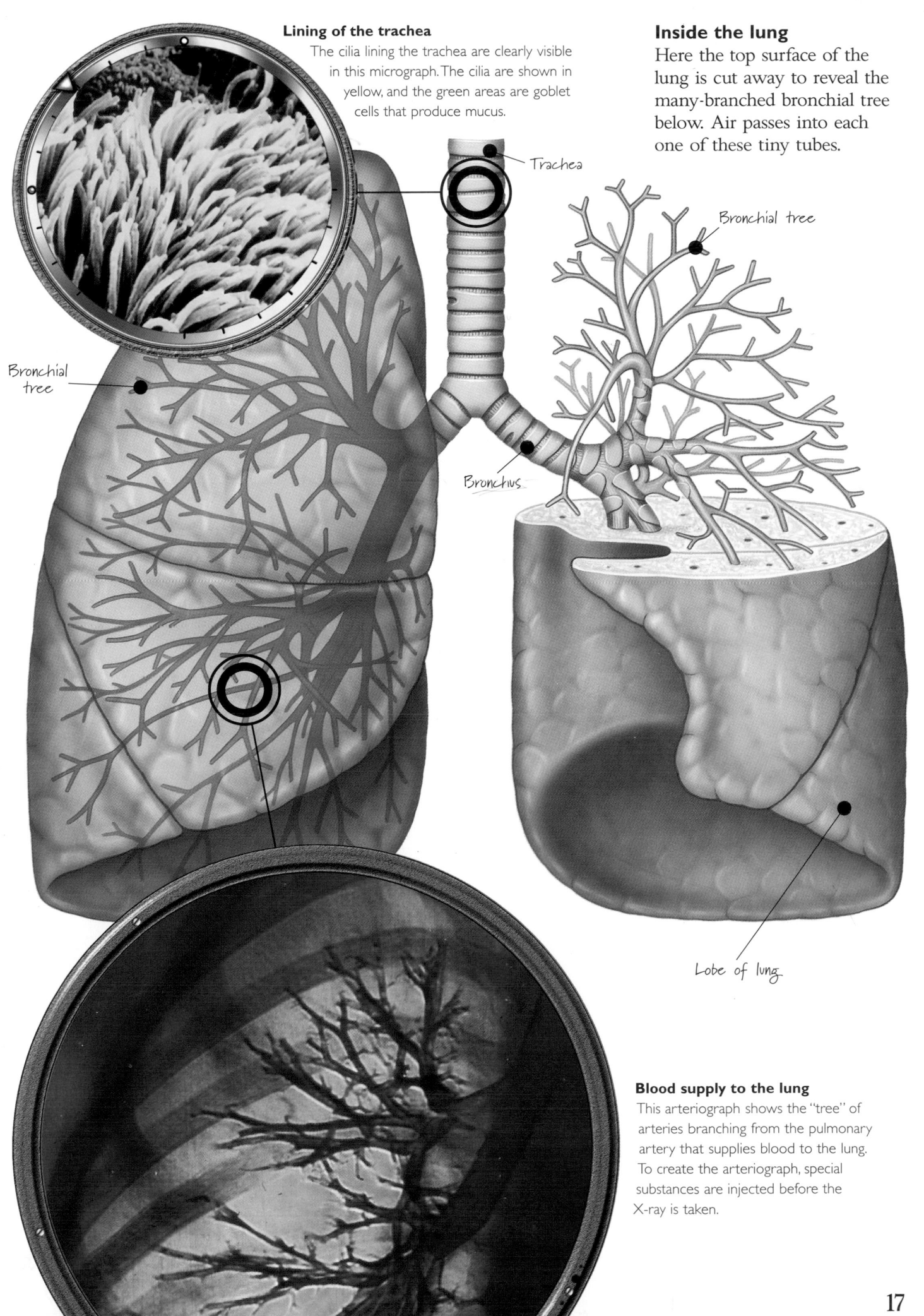

**Lining of the trachea**

The cilia lining the trachea are clearly visible in this micrograph. The cilia are shown in yellow, and the green areas are goblet cells that produce mucus.

**Inside the lung**

Here the top surface of the lung is cut away to reveal the many-branched bronchial tree below. Air passes into each one of these tiny tubes.

Trachea

Bronchial tree

Bronchial tree

Bronchus

Lobe of lung

**Blood supply to the lung**

This arteriograph shows the "tree" of arteries branching from the pulmonary artery that supplies blood to the lung. To create the arteriograph, special substances are injected before the X-ray is taken.

# THE LUNGS

The lungs are two spongy organs that fill most of the chest. They are protected by the bony cage formed by the ribs. The lungs are filled with the many-branched tubes of the bronchial tree.

Deep furrows in the surface of the lungs divide them into different parts called lobes. The right lung has three lobes. The left lung shares the left side of the chest with the heart and so has only two lobes.

The lungs are surrounded by two membranes. The inner membrane is attached to the lungs, and the outer to the inside of the ribs. The space between the membranes is filled with a thin film of fluid. This helps the lungs move inside the rib cage during breathing.

Blood is pumped into the lungs from the heart through the pulmonary arteries. The arteries branch like the bronchial tubes, creating a network that carries blood to all parts of the lungs. Oxygenated blood leaves the lungs through the pulmonary veins and travels to the heart. From here it is pumped around the body.

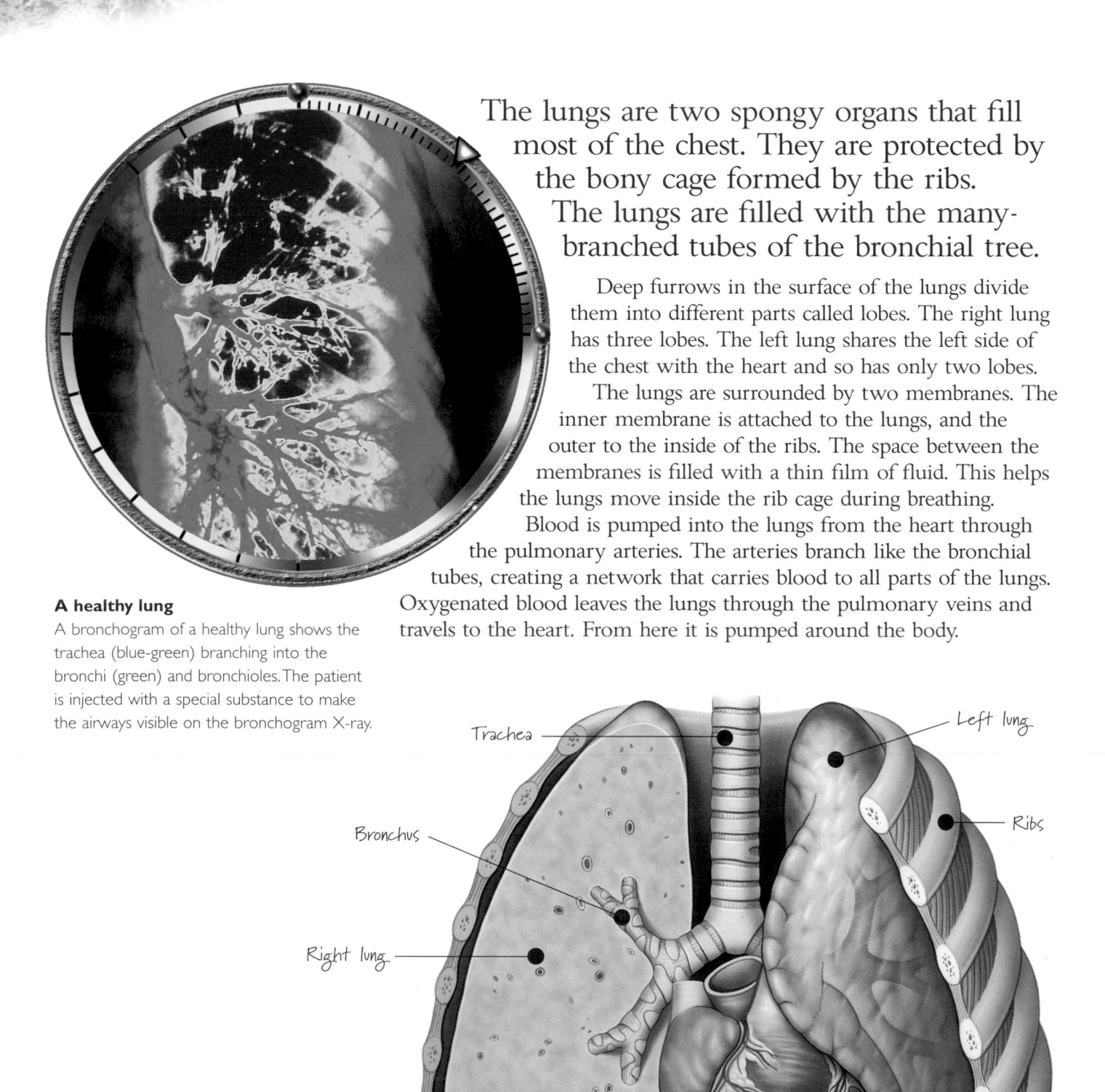

**A healthy lung**
A bronchogram of a healthy lung shows the trachea (blue-green) branching into the bronchi (green) and bronchioles. The patient is injected with a special substance to make the airways visible on the bronchogram X-ray.

Trachea

Left lung

Bronchus

Ribs

Right lung

Heart

**A view inside the chest**
A cutaway of the front of the chest shows the relative positions of the heart and lungs within the chest. All of these delicate organs are enclosed by the rib cage. The right lung is shown as a section, revealing its spongy texture and the main bronchi.

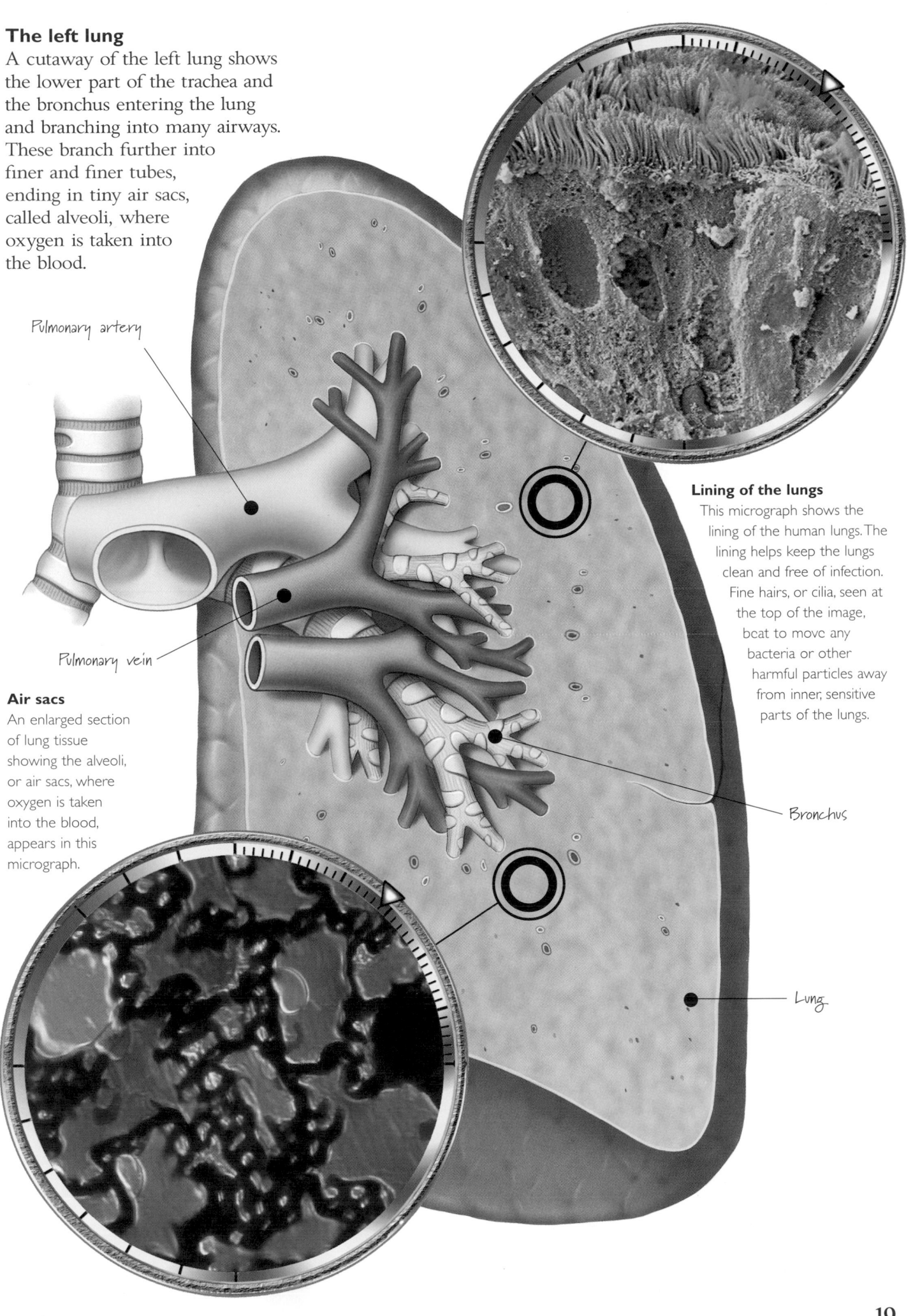

## The left lung

A cutaway of the left lung shows the lower part of the trachea and the bronchus entering the lung and branching into many airways. These branch further into finer and finer tubes, ending in tiny air sacs, called alveoli, where oxygen is taken into the blood.

Pulmonary artery

Pulmonary vein

### Air sacs

An enlarged section of lung tissue showing the alveoli, or air sacs, where oxygen is taken into the blood, appears in this micrograph.

### Lining of the lungs

This micrograph shows the lining of the human lungs. The lining helps keep the lungs clean and free of infection. Fine hairs, or cilia, seen at the top of the image, beat to move any bacteria or other harmful particles away from inner, sensitive parts of the lungs.

Bronchus

Lung

# HOW WE BREATHE

Breathing involves the ribs, the intercostal muscles, and the diaphragm as well as the lungs.

Before breathing in, the muscles attached to the ribs, called the intercostals, contract. The ribs move outward, and the diaphragm flattens. These movements increase the size of the chest cavity and allow air to rush into the lungs.

When breathing out, the muscles relax, the ribs go back to their normal unexpanded position, and the diaphragm springs back into place. With the chest cavity back to its normal size, air is forced out of the lungs, through the upper respiratory organs, and out of the nose or mouth.

But when we breathe out, the lungs do not empty completely. Blood is constantly flowing through the lungs on its journey around the body, so there must always be some oxygen there for it to pick up. Even if you breathe out as hard as you can, the lungs will still be about one-fifth filled with air.

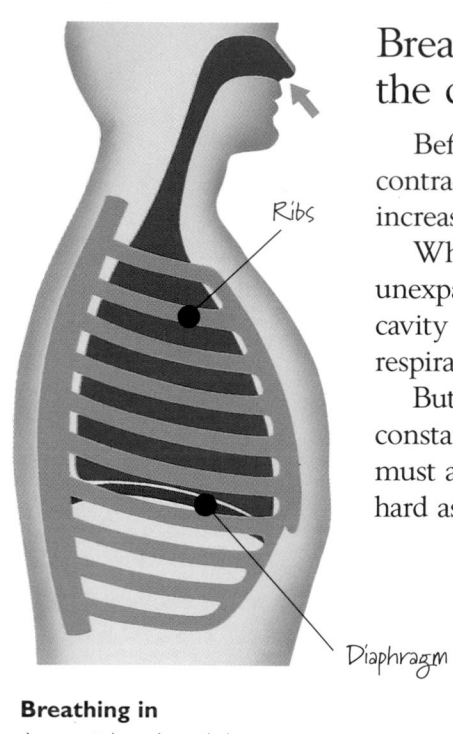

Ribs

Diaphragm

**Breathing in**
As you take a breath in, your diaphragm flattens and the ribs expand outward and upward. This makes the chest cavity bigger.

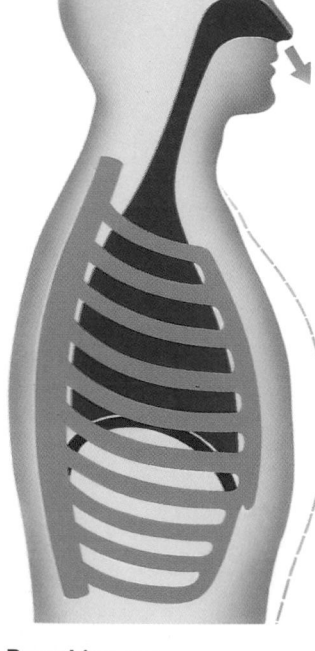

**Breathing out**
As you breathe out, the ribs and diaphragm go back to their normal positions.

Brain

Breathing center

Brain stem

**Breathing control**
Breathing is controlled automatically by a respiratory center in the brain stem at the base of the brain. This center receives information about, for example, how much carbon dioxide is in the blood. It then sends out instructions to the rib muscles and diaphragm to speed up or slow down breathing.

**Take a deep breath**
Before blowing up a balloon or an inflatable toy,
you take a deep breath in order to fill your lungs
with as much air as possible. An adult's lungs
could hold about 12 pints (6,000 milliliters) of air.

# GAS EXCHANGE

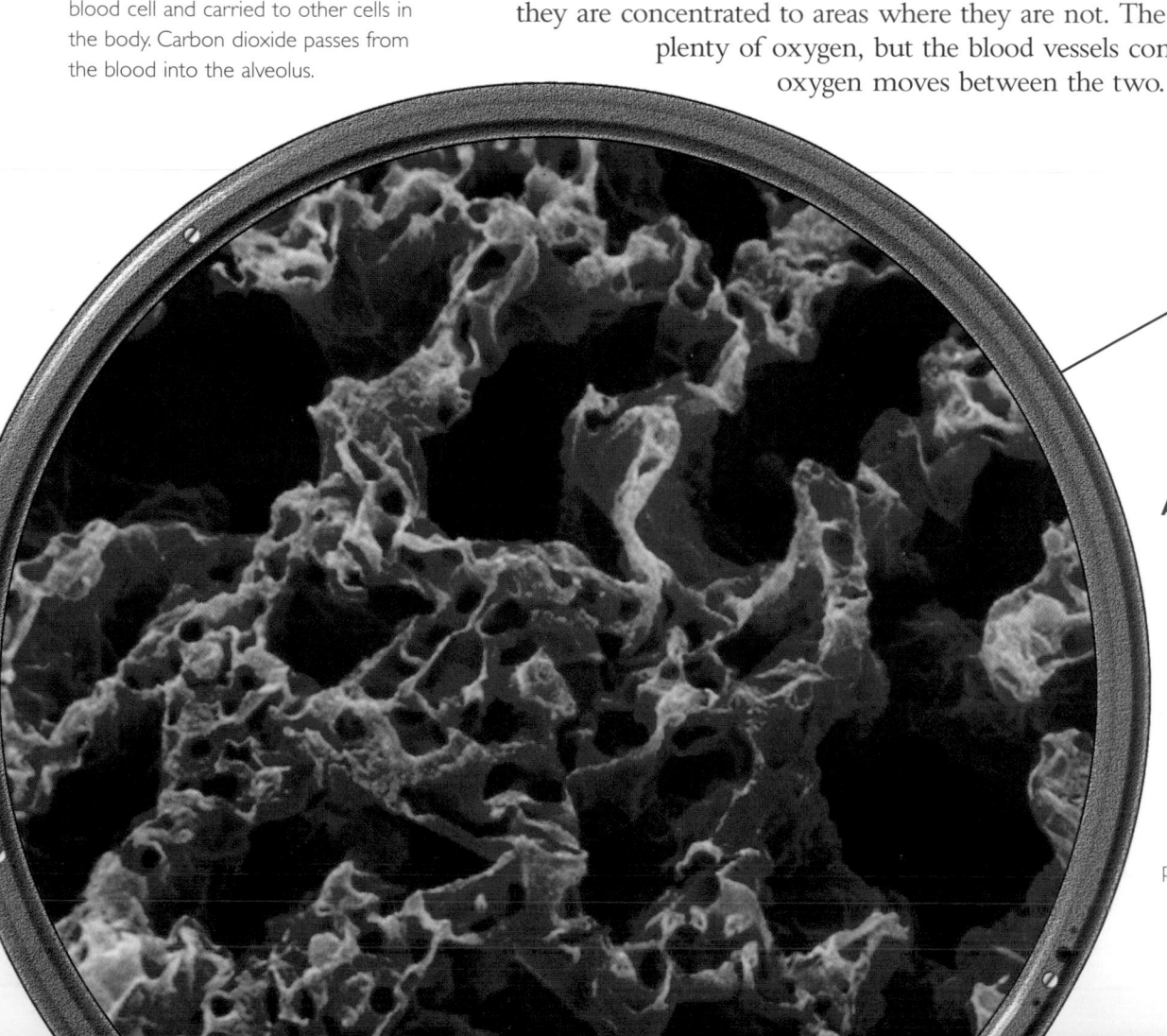

Breathing in and out of the lungs is only part of the story of respiration. The next stage is the process by which oxygen passes into the blood and is carried in the blood to body cells.

Air flows into the lungs and into all the tiny tubes called bronchioles. Each bronchiole ends in a cluster of alveoli, air sacs that look like bunches of tiny balloons. It is here that what is called "gas exchange" takes place.

Each alveolus is surrounded by tiny, thin-walled blood vessels called capillaries. Oxygen passes through the thin walls of the alveolus into the blood vessel. At the same time, carbon dioxide passes from the blood into the alveolus and is breathed out from the lungs. This is gas exchange. The oxygenated blood is carried to the heart, from where it is pumped around the body to give the cells the oxygen they need to function.

But why does the oxygen pass out of the alveolus into the blood vessel? This is mainly because gases naturally move from areas where they are concentrated to areas where they are not. The alveolus contains plenty of oxygen, but the blood vessels contain little, so oxygen moves between the two.

**How gas exchange works**

Oxygen passes through the membrane enclosing the alveolus into a blood vessel or capillary. Here it is taken up by a red blood cell and carried to other cells in the body. Carbon dioxide passes from the blood into the alveolus.

**Air spaces**

The spaces in the mesh of lung tissue shown in this micrograph are the alveoli, or air sacs. Their walls are extremely thin so that oxygen can pass out of them into the blood, and carbon dioxide can pass into them.

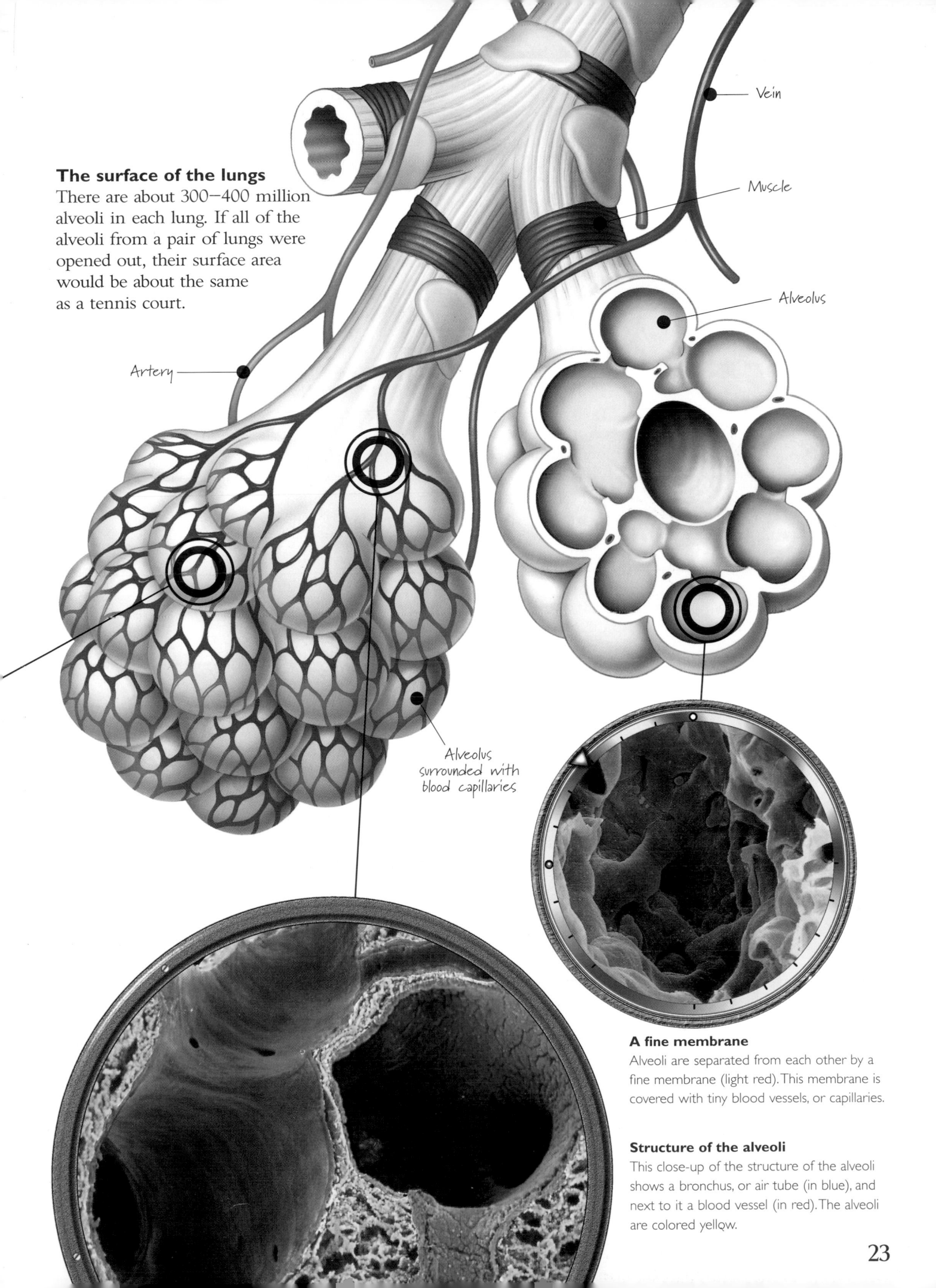

**The surface of the lungs**

There are about 300–400 million alveoli in each lung. If all of the alveoli from a pair of lungs were opened out, their surface area would be about the same as a tennis court.

Vein

Muscle

Alveolus

Artery

Alveolus surrounded with blood capillaries

**A fine membrane**

Alveoli are separated from each other by a fine membrane (light red). This membrane is covered with tiny blood vessels, or capillaries.

**Structure of the alveoli**

This close-up of the structure of the alveoli shows a bronchus, or air tube (in blue), and next to it a blood vessel (in red). The alveoli are colored yellow.

# THE FIRST BREATH

**The beginnings of life**
Even though this five-week-old embryo is only about ½ inch (15 millimeters) long, the vital organs, such as the heart and lungs, are already starting to form.

The lungs and other parts of the respiratory system start to form when a baby in the womb is only a few weeks old and less than 1 inch (2.5 centimeters) long.

Development is complete by 28 weeks. The baby cannot breathe air while inside the mother's womb, but it does need oxygen. It gets this from its mother through the placenta, its life-support system within the womb. The umbilical cord, which links the baby with the placenta, brings oxygen and takes away waste, such as carbon dioxide. The oxygenated blood in the umbilical cord flows straight to the baby's heart, from where it is pumped around its body.

At birth everything changes, and the baby must breathe for itself as soon as it emerges from the womb. As soon as it takes its first breath, the circulation pattern alters, and the full respiratory system begins to operate. The first few breaths are difficult, as the lungs are filled with the fluid that kept them inflated in the womb. This fluid is soon taken up by the bloodstream and expelled from the body.

**First breath**
A baby's loud cry immediately after birth is a signal that it has taken its first breath. It takes a few days for the breathing pattern to settle down. Babies breathe faster than adults. They take as many as 30-40 breaths a minute.

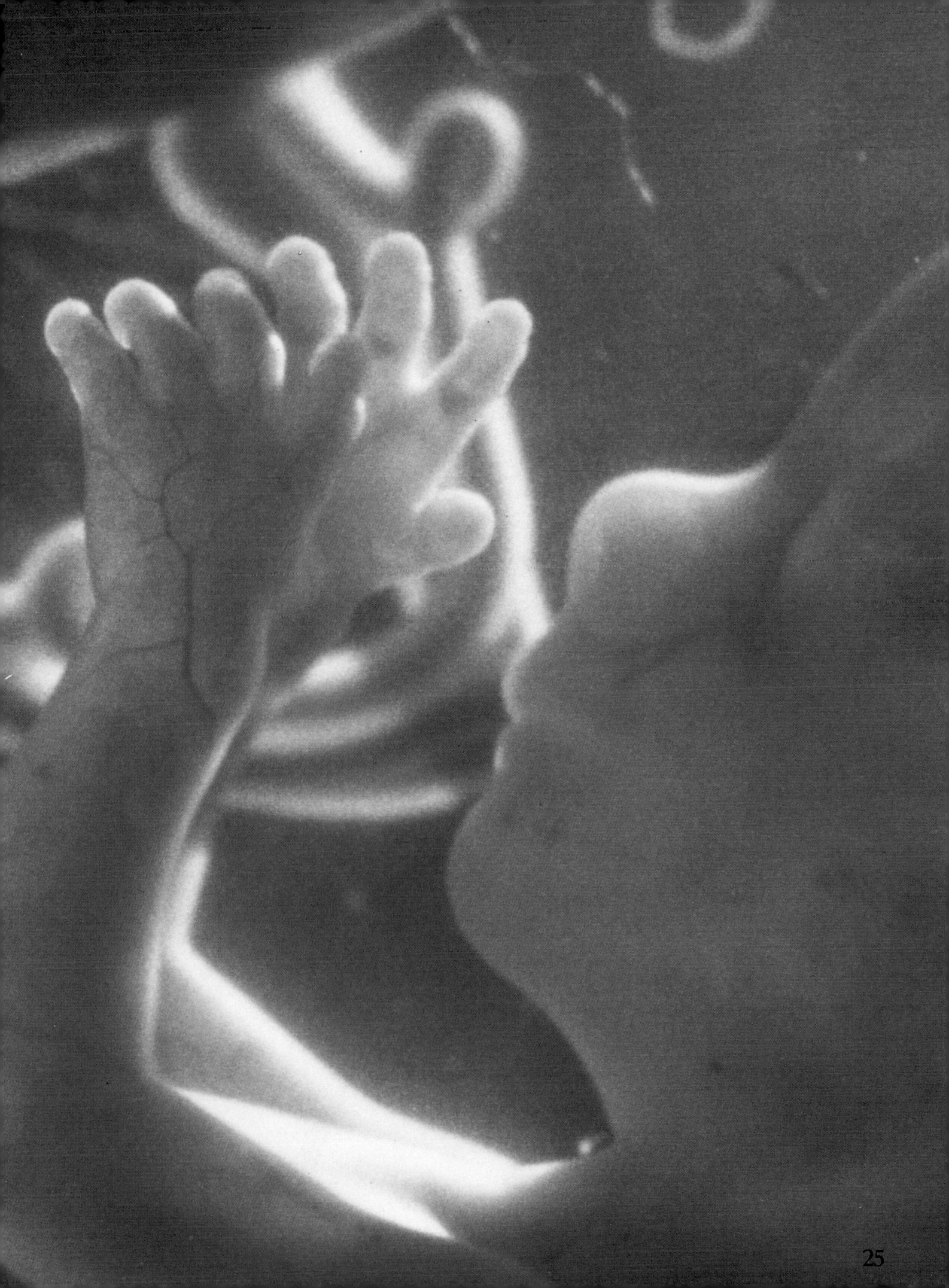

# BREATHING NOISES

**Out of breath**
After a strenuous race even the fittest athlete is out of breath. He needs to breathe fast for a few minutes to replace the extra oxygen used to fuel the body while running.

Normally breathing is a quiet process. But there are certain adaptations of the breathing process that do make sounds. Each has a particular purpose. When we need more oxygen than usual, for example, when running, we breathe in and out faster and more heavily, making the familiar sound called panting.

Yawning, on the other hand, is the body's reaction to too much carbon dioxide having built up in the lungs. The mouth opens wide to draw in an extra big breath and more oxygen. Why seeing someone yawn makes other people want to do it too is not understood.

Coughing and sneezing are fast-moving rushes of air that clear irritation or blockages from the respiratory system. Irritating though they may be, they are an important safety mechanism for the respiratory system. A hiccup is also a response to some form of irritation or disruption of the system. The diaphragm suddenly contracts, and as air is breathed in, the vocal cords close together, making the familiar "hic" sound.

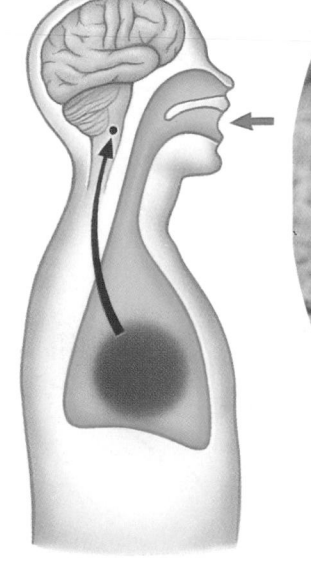

**A big yawn**
Too much carbon dioxide in the body can cause us to yawn. The breathing control center tells us to take in an extra big breath through a wide open mouth to get more oxygen.

**Making music**
Wind instruments, such as flutes and didgeridoos, produce sounds when air is blown into them by the player. The length and shape of the instrument and the type of mouthpiece affect the tone and pitch of the sound made.

**Fast-moving air**

When you laugh, sneeze, cough, or hiccup, air moves out of the body faster than usual. As you laugh, for example, air moves at 15 mph (25 kilometers an hour). Coughing and hiccuping move air faster still, and the air in a sneeze moves at an amazing 100 mph (160 kilometers an hour). A yawn is much slower — in a yawning breath air moves at only about 9 mph (15 kilometers an hour).

# BREATHING & EXERCISE

When you exercise or do any vigorous activity, your muscles have to work much harder. They need more oxygen than when you are resting or sitting still. Your breathing speeds up to get more oxygen into the body, and your heart rate increases to pump more oxygenated blood around the body.

For example, when you are asleep or sitting quietly, you may breathe about 12 to 14 times a minute. But if you run fast, you may breathe twice as fast as this and take in at least five times more air to cope with the body's demands.

There are two sorts of exercise: aerobic and anaerobic. Aerobic exercise is continuous activity over a period of time, such as jogging, swimming, or even fast walking. The body needs plenty of oxygen to fuel the exercise, and we breathe deeper and faster to obtain it. But the activity is not so vigorous that we get completely out of breath and have to stop.

Anaerobic exercise is a short burst of extremely high-speed activity such as sprinting. There is not time for extra oxygen to get to the muscles, so energy is released quickly without oxygen. When the activity is over, you continue to breathe fast for a while.

**Quiet breathing**
When you are simply sitting quietly, reading a book, or just thinking, you take about 12-14 breaths a minute.

**Asleep and breathing**
You breathe all the time, even when you are asleep. As you sleep, you take about 12-14 breaths a minute.

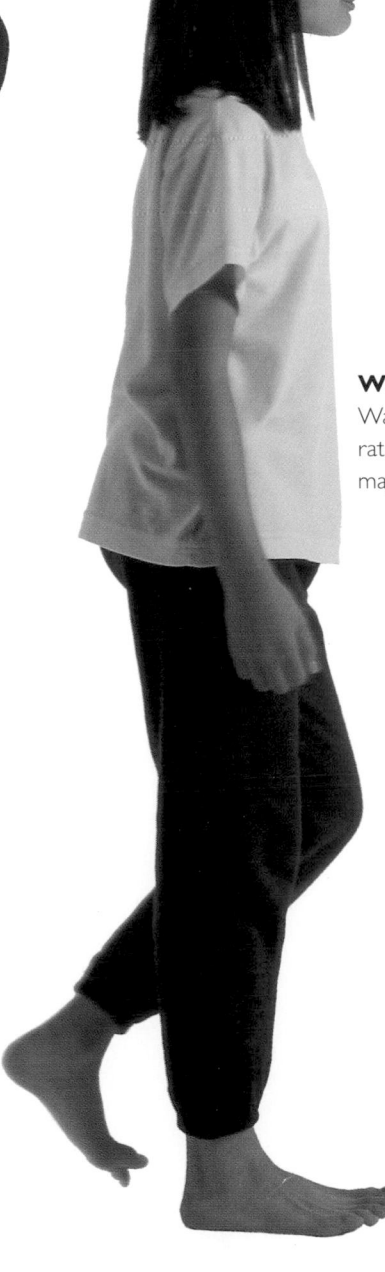

### Oxygen supply

This micrograph shows a close-up of a blood capillary (shown in blue) in a muscle (red). The blood must keep up a constant supply of oxygen to the muscle cells.

### Walking

Walking uses extra energy, so the breathing rate speeds up to fuel the body's needs. You may breathe about 20 times a minute.

### Running

Now your body must work really hard, and you may need to take as many as 30 breaths a minute.

# BREATHING UNDERWATER

Fish are specially adapted to obtain oxygen from water instead of air. A fish takes water into its mouth, where it flows over structures called gills. Oxygen passes from the water into the blood flowing through the gills and is then pumped around the body by the heart.

Humans, like other mammals, cannot take oxygen from water. We have to hold our breath when we dive under the surface or breathe through special equipment. The simplest breathing equipment is a snorkel. But this cannot work below 18 inches (45 centimeters) deep, because the pressure of the water is too great. The diver would be unable to move his or her chest. For deeper dives divers wear scuba equipment.

## Breathing underwater

Instead of lungs to take oxygen from air, a fish has gills that extract oxygen from water. The gills are positioned at the sides of the fish's head and are covered by a protective flap. Out of water a fish quickly dies from lack of oxygen.

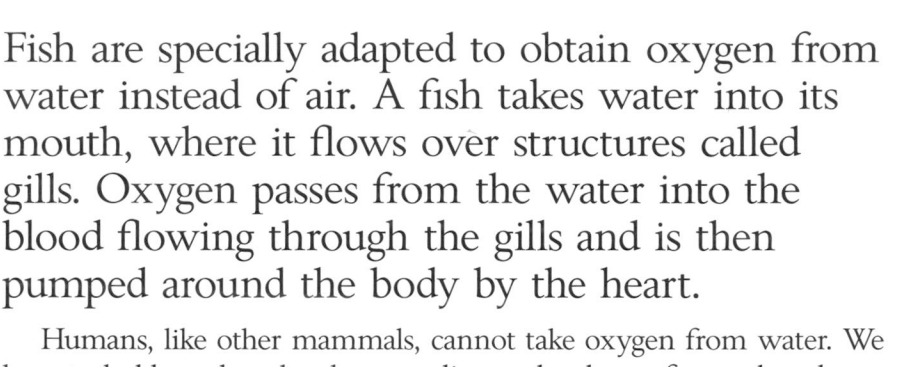

*Gills covered by protective flap*

## A fish's gills

When the fish opens its mouth, water flows in. Because the throat is closed off, the water is forced over the gills, where oxygen is removed. The gill flaps open, and the water flows back out. The gills are made of lots of tightly packed plates called lamellae. Like lungs, they have a large surface area if opened out.

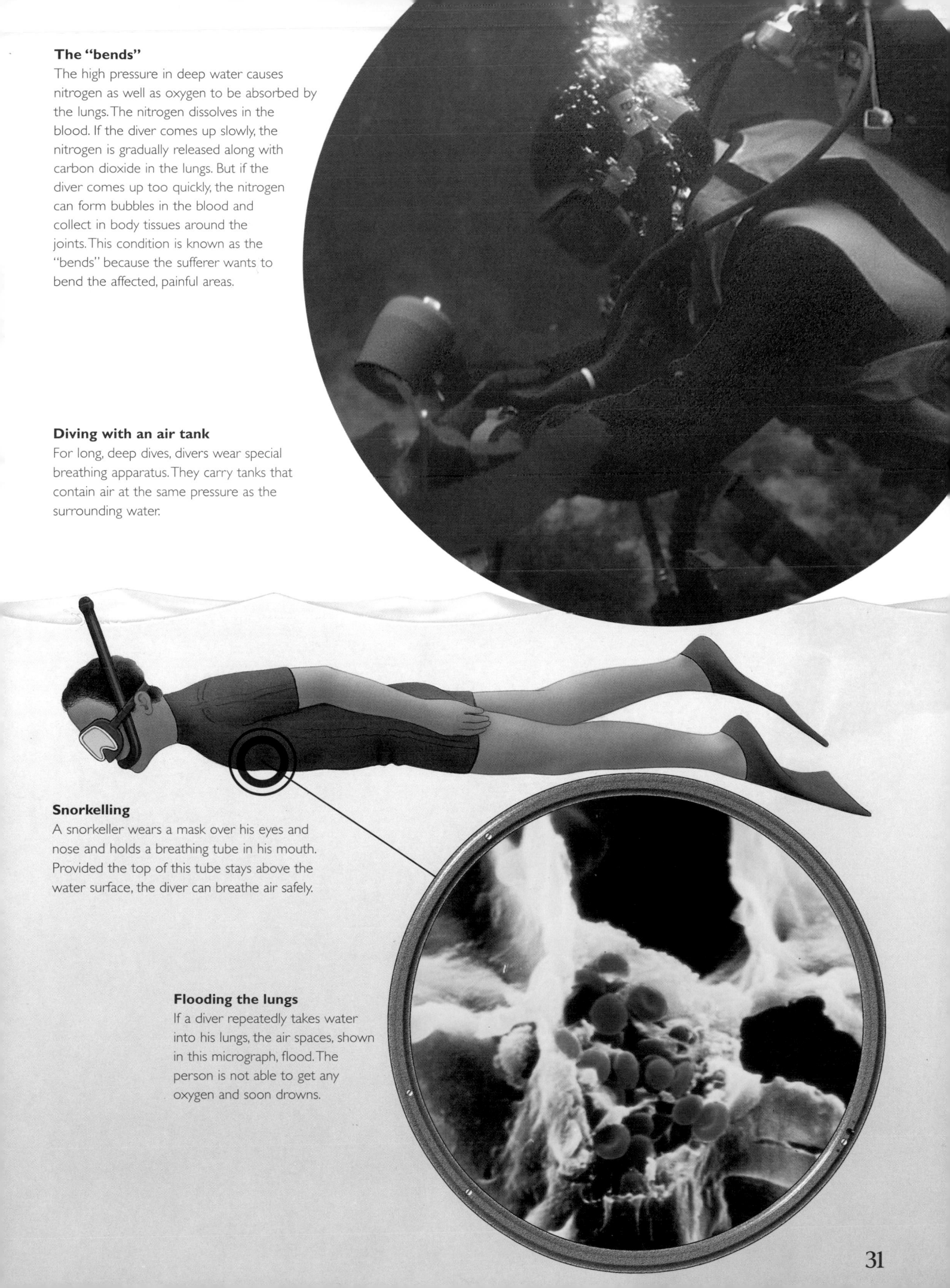

### The "bends"

The high pressure in deep water causes nitrogen as well as oxygen to be absorbed by the lungs. The nitrogen dissolves in the blood. If the diver comes up slowly, the nitrogen is gradually released along with carbon dioxide in the lungs. But if the diver comes up too quickly, the nitrogen can form bubbles in the blood and collect in body tissues around the joints. This condition is known as the "bends" because the sufferer wants to bend the affected, painful areas.

### Diving with an air tank

For long, deep dives, divers wear special breathing apparatus. They carry tanks that contain air at the same pressure as the surrounding water.

### Snorkelling

A snorkeller wears a mask over his eyes and nose and holds a breathing tube in his mouth. Provided the top of this tube stays above the water surface, the diver can breathe air safely.

### Flooding the lungs

If a diver repeatedly takes water into his lungs, the air spaces, shown in this micrograph, flood. The person is not able to get any oxygen and soon drowns.

# BREATHING AT ALTITUDE

**Life masks**
Pilots flying planes at high altitudes have to wear a mask that supplies them with air. Without the mask strapped firmly in place they would become unconscious and lose control of the plane.

While pressure increases the deeper underwater you go, making it hard to breathe, pressure decreases the higher you are above sea level. This also makes breathing difficult.

At high altitudes atmospheric pressure is less, and the air becomes thinner. The gases in the air are literally more spread out, and there is less oxygen in every breath you take. Climbers to the world's highest peaks generally carry tanks of pressurized air, though some have made it to the top of Mount Everest without breathing equipment. Such climbers need gradually to get used to higher altitudes to give their bodies time to adjust. Altitude sickness can be extremely severe, and even experienced climbers have died from its effects.

The human body, however, is very adaptable, and some mountain people have adjusted to life at high altitude. Such people have more red blood cells than normal, so can carry oxygen more efficiently.

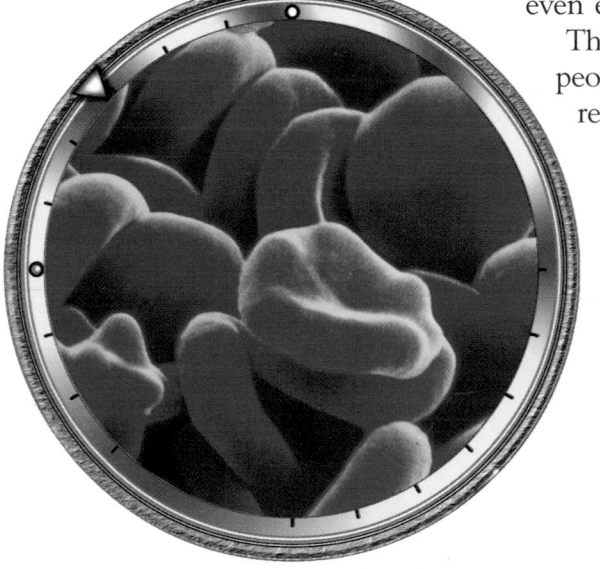

**Red blood cells**
People used to living at high altitude gradually adapt to the conditions. Their blood contains a higher than normal proportion of oxygen-carrying red blood cells. This micrograph shows greatly magnified red blood cells.

**Mountain people**
The human body is extremely adaptable, and some mountain people have adjusted to the difficulties of breathing at high altitude. In Peru thousands of people live in villages more than 13,000 feet (4,000 meters) up in the Andes mountains.

### Breathing in space

There is no atmosphere in space so astronauts must be provided with air. Inside the space capsule they breathe supplies of pressurized air. Astronauts leaving the spacecraft for space walks take air tanks. These generally contain 100 percent oxygen at lower than normal pressure.

### A pressurized cabin

Airplanes fly higher than the highest mountains, and without pressurized cabins passengers could not survive. Cabins are pressurized to the equivalent of about 6,500 feet (2,000 meters) above sea level so that passengers can breathe comfortably.

### Altitude training

Most climbers need to use breathing apparatus above 16,400 feet (5,000 meters), but the body can make some adjustments to low oxygen levels. Climbers train by gradually getting used to life at higher and higher levels. Ideally they should make their climbs slowly, with regular stops at base camps so their bodies can get used to the conditions.

# FRESH AIR & POLLUTION

**Fighting pollution**
Carbon monoxide and hydrocarbons from cars can make cycling in busy city streets very unpleasant. More and more cyclists are wearing masks in an effort to protect themselves from pollution. But a mask only protects the wearer from the largest sooty particles and cannot stop harmful gases or tiny particles from entering the lungs.

The respiratory system makes every effort to keep itself clean and avoid dirt and pollutants in the air. Tiny hairs in the nose catch large foreign bodies. Mucus in the nose and throat catches more dirt and bacteria.

If anything gets down to the lower part of the system, it is pushed out by the hairs lining the larger bronchi. Tiny particles that may reach the alveoli are dealt with by special scavenger cells called macrophages.

Despite all of this, some minute particles in polluted air manage to cause damage to the lungs. Little pieces of coal dust, silicon, asbestos, and cotton fiber may be breathed in by people working with these substances and cause severe illness. Those dealing with radioactive minerals may inhale radioactive dust. And we are all at risk from the gaseous pollutants, such as hydrocarbons and sulfur and nitrogen oxides, given off by some factories and by motor vehicles. These can cause breathing difficulties and severe discomfort for those suffering from illnesses such as asthma and bronchitis.

Efforts are being made to control pollutants and make air cleaner, but each year there are more and more cars on the road and larger industrialized areas. Air moves anywhere and everywhere, so this is a worldwide problem. The United Nations World Health Organization monitors air pollution and is working toward cleaner air, but it is a constant and ever more difficult battle.

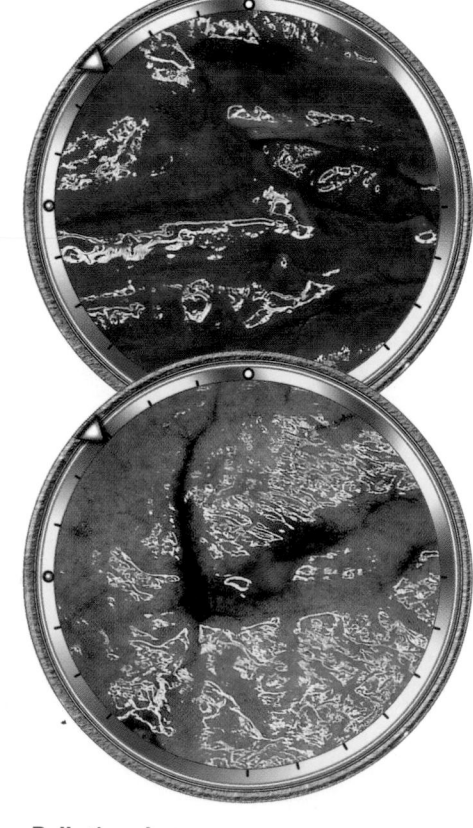

**Fresh air?**
Being out in the fresh air in a beautiful country landscape (right) is health-giving. But too many places are becoming clogged with industrial pollution belching from factory chimneys (far right).

**Pollution damage**
The top picture here shows the inside of a normal healthy bronchus, or airway, in a human lung. But the picture below it shows the inside of a bronchus badly affected by pollution. The black areas are deposits of soot from polluted air.

34

**Polluting the air**
Some industries spew out polluting
particles and gases from chimneys, which
seriously affect air quality. Such polluted
air is harmful to all who breathe it, but it
can be particularly dangerous for those
already suffering from respiratory diseases
such as asthma.

# SMOKING

Smoking, once thought to be a harmless social habit, has been clearly linked with a number of serious illnesses, including lung cancer, bronchitis, and heart disease.

Cigarette smoke contains carbon monoxide and other poisonous chemicals that harm the body, especially the lungs. Smoking also makes the heart beat faster because it has to do more work to get enough oxygen to the cells.

Many of the particles in cigarette smoke are too small to be trapped in the respiratory system's defenses of cilia and mucus, and so they enter the lungs. The smoke damages the cilia, causing them to beat more slowly and be less efficient. At the same time, it damages the macrophages that attack smoke particles that reach the alveoli.

As the smoke particles cool, they form sticky tar that settles in the lungs and can cause lung cancer. The carbon monoxide in cigarette smoke can cross the membrane of alveoli just like oxygen. It enters the blood cells and prevents them taking in enough oxygen. This makes it harder to get enough oxygen to cells, and the smoker's health suffers.

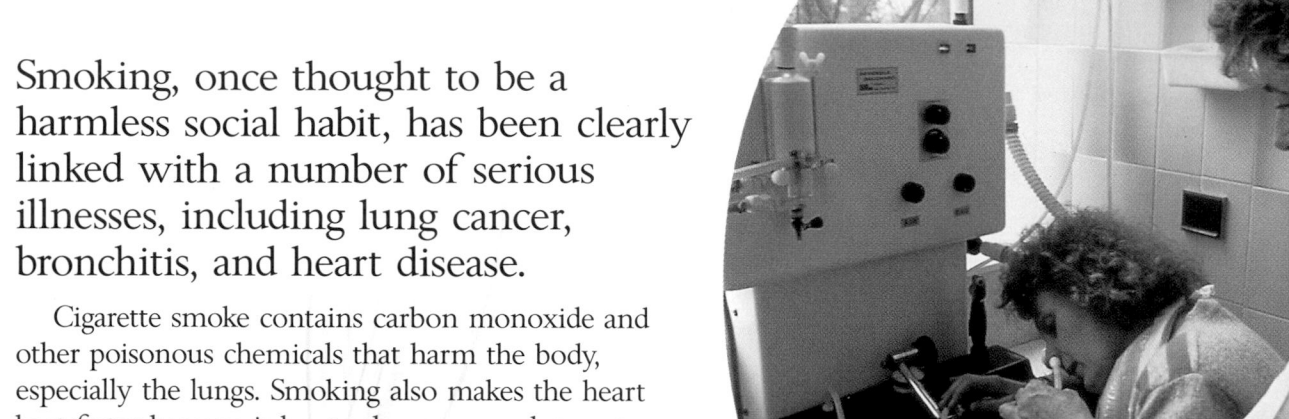

**Kicking the habit**
Many methods are used to wean people off smoking cigarettes. Cigarette smoke contains the drug nicotine, which is very addictive. This makes it hard for people to give up the deadly habit.

**A dangerous habit**
Doctors think that smoking is the cause of about 30 percent of all cancer deaths. It can also cause heart problems and diseases such as bronchitis and emphysema.

**Tar on the lung**
The dark patches on this close-up of a section of a smoker's lung are deposits of sticky tar caused by cigarette smoke.

**Smoke damage**
When we are born, our lungs are pink and healthy. As we grow older, they usually become darker in color, and some dirt particles gather. Compare the reasonably healthy lungs of a nonsmoker, right, with the lungs of a smoker, above. The smoker's lungs have become severely discolored and pitted with sticky tars. The smoke irritates the airways, causing them to become inflamed and thickened, and damages the air sacs, or alveoli, where gas exchange takes place.

# RESPIRATORY ILLNESSES

Because we breathe in so many bacteria and viruses with the air, our respiratory system is very vulnerable to illness. The most common respiratory illnesses are colds and influenza. They are caused by different sorts of virus that make cells in the nose and throat swell and produce more mucus than usual.

Another common illness is bronchitis, in which the membranes lining the bronchial tubes become inflamed. Lots of thick mucus is produced, and the patient develops a nasty cough in efforts to get rid of it. Acute bronchitis caused by bacteria can last for some weeks, but chronic bronchitis as a result of smoking or breathing polluted air can continue as long as the irritant is present.

Emphysema is also caused by long-term smoking. As in bronchitis, the lungs produce a lot of mucus, and the alveoli are stretched and begin to sag. It becomes harder and harder for sufferers to breathe and get enough oxygen, and the slightest activity makes them breathless.

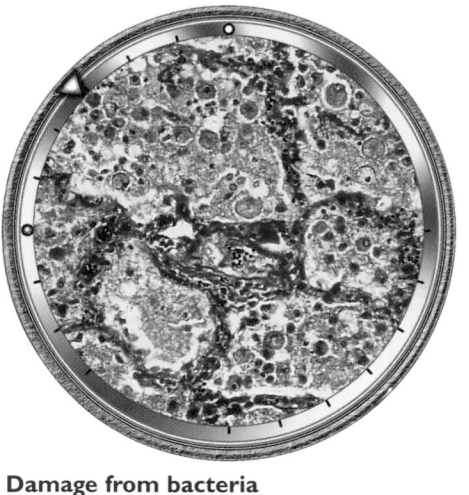

**Damage from bacteria**
An airway in a person suffering from pneumonia is shown in this micrograph. The airways and alveoli have been damaged by the spread of the bacteria in the lungs.

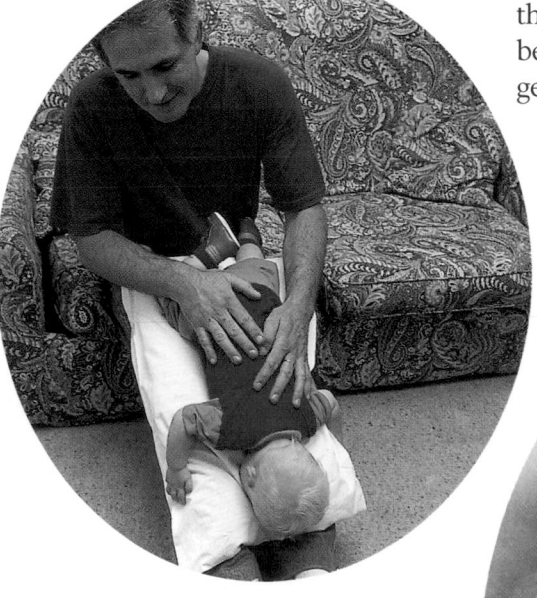

**An inherited illness**
Cystic fibrosis is a different kind of respiratory disease. It is genetic, which means it is inherited from a parent. The sufferer produces extra thick secretions of sweat, mucus, and other fluids. Airways become blocked and infected, making breathing difficult. There is no cure for this condition at present, but drug treatment and massage make life more comfortable.

**Spreading the virus**
A special photographic technique called Schlieren photography shows the stream of air and droplets that explodes from the lungs when someone coughs. Some of these may contain the virus causing the cough, and so the infection spreads.

## A disease carried in water

Deadly legionnaire's disease is caused by bacteria carried in water. The disease can be contracted through faulty air-conditioning systems. Below are two views of the bacteria that cause the disease.

## Pneumonia

This colored X-ray shows the lungs of a patient suffering from a particular kind of pneumonia that begins in a lobe of the lungs. The affected area is shown in pink. As the illness worsens, the airways become blocked and breathing is painful. The patient can be cured with antibiotics.

# ALLERGIES

Some people have airways that are highly sensitive, or allergic, to certain substances. A very common allergic condition is hay fever. Sufferers are usually sensitive to the pollen of trees and grasses in spring and summer, and the allergic reaction causes coldlike symptoms, such as sneezing, eye irritation, and other discomforts.

Asthma is another respiratory disorder that can be triggered by allergies to pollen, dust mites, animal hairs, and other substances. These cause chemical reactions in the airways that make the muscles in the walls of the airways contract, bringing on an asthma attack. Inflammation and the extra mucus produced make the airways narrower still. There is not enough room for air to flow properly through the narrowed passages, and the sufferer breathes with great difficulty, making wheezing sounds.

Asthmatics can inhale medicines that relax the muscles of the airways and make breathing easier, but attacks are still unpleasant. Not all asthma is caused by allergies, however. Stress and psychological factors are among the other triggers for attacks.

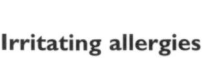

**Relieving symptoms**

Asthma sufferers carry inhalers containing drugs to relieve their symptoms. They breathe in a medicated mist that relaxes the muscles of the airways and improves air flow. In severe attacks sufferers may need to be taken to hospital to receive oxygen and other treatment.

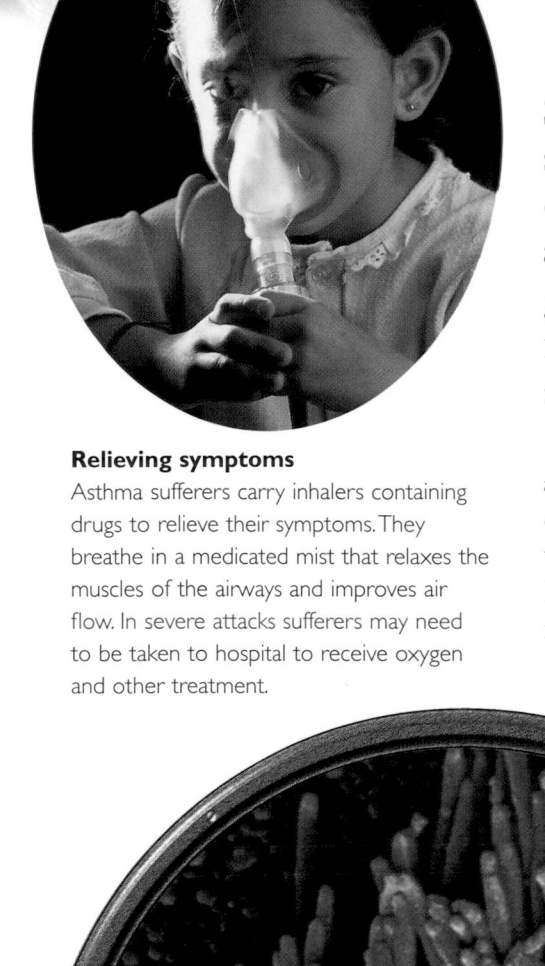

**Irritating allergies**

An allergy to pollen causes inflammation and irritation in the nose. This micrograph shows how the cilia in the nose have lengthened due to the irritation.

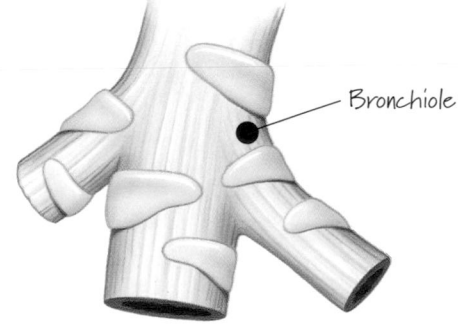

Bronchiole

**Narrowed airways**

The muscles in the walls of a normal bronchiole are relaxed. There is plenty of room for air to pass comfortably through the tube. During an asthma attack the muscles in the walls of the bronchiole contract, making the space narrower. Mucus collects and makes it narrower still.

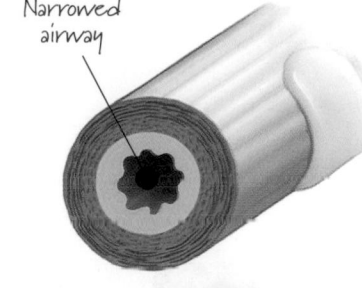

Narrowed airway

Normal airway

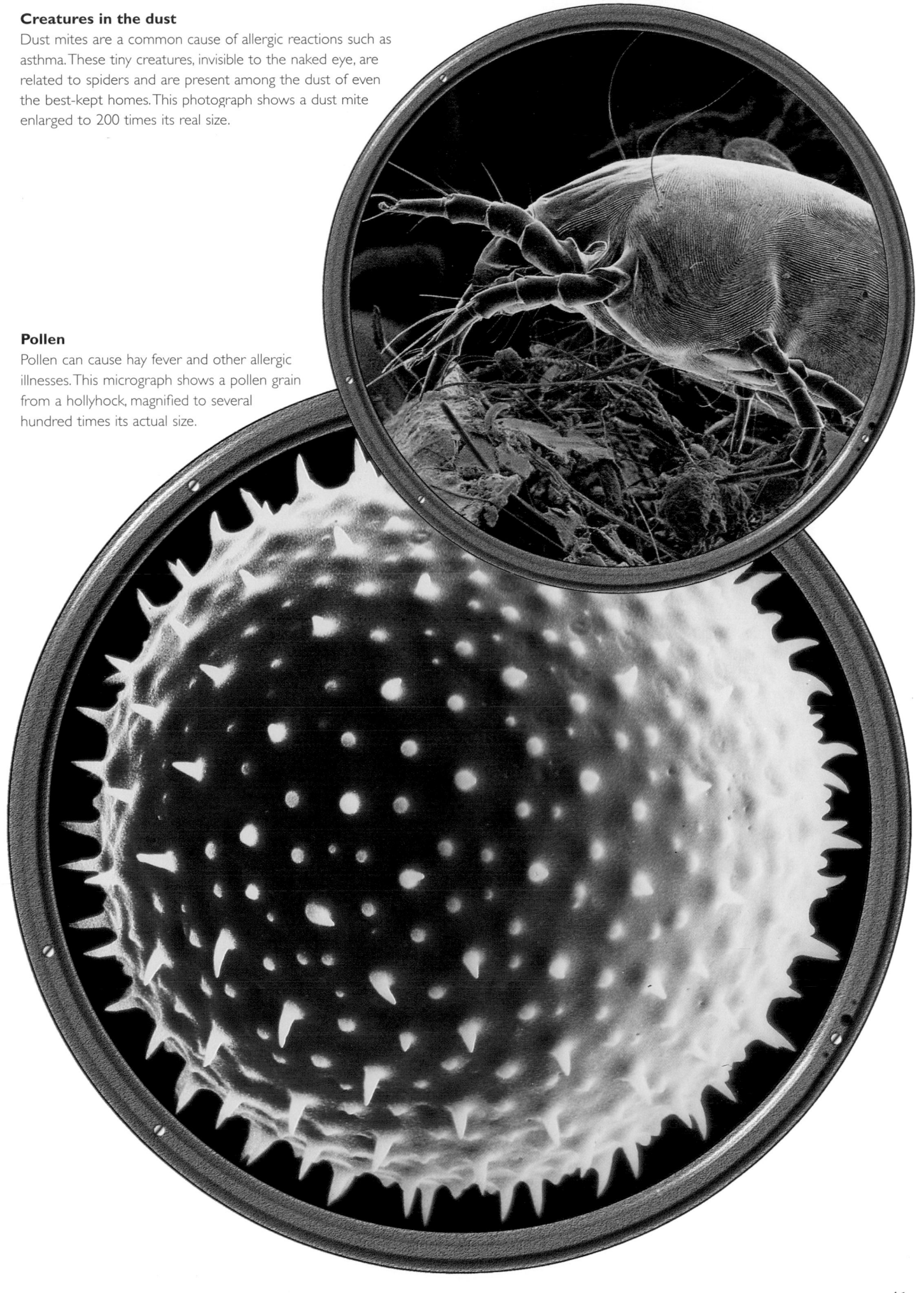

**Creatures in the dust**

Dust mites are a common cause of allergic reactions such as asthma. These tiny creatures, invisible to the naked eye, are related to spiders and are present among the dust of even the best-kept homes. This photograph shows a dust mite enlarged to 200 times its real size.

**Pollen**

Pollen can cause hay fever and other allergic illnesses. This micrograph shows a pollen grain from a hollyhock, magnified to several hundred times its actual size.

# ANESTHESIA & LIFE SUPPORT

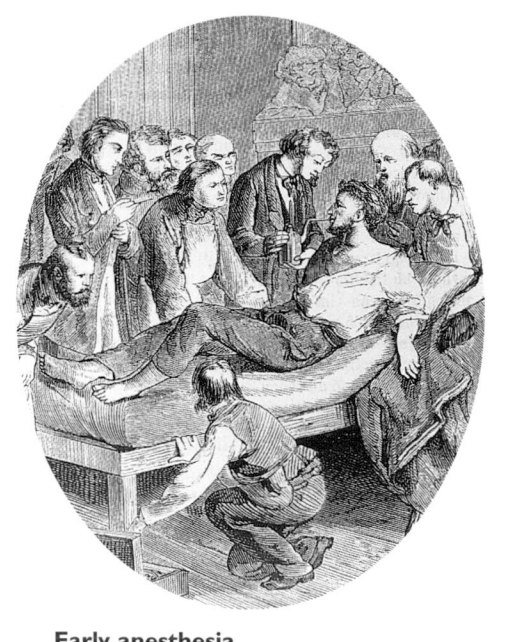

**Early anesthesia**
The first surgical operation under anesthetic is shown in this engraving. Surgeons operated in 1846 at a hospital in Massachusetts to remove a tumor from a patient's neck.

Anesthesia is a process by which patients about to have an operation are given substances that make them lose consciousness and feel no pain. Without it surgeons could not do their work.

Before anesthetics were developed, doctors tried giving their patients lots of alcohol or narcotic drugs, such as opium, to dull the pain of surgery. Then in the 19th century dentists and surgeons started asking patients to inhale different gases, such as ether, nitrous oxide, and chloroform. These did make the patient lose consciousness, but breathing in the strong-smelling gases was not a pleasant experience.

Today patients have an injection that puts them to sleep before they are a given a combination of gases to inhale. These work on the nervous system, making the person unconscious and stopping them feeling any pain. During chest operations a patient may also be given drugs to relax the muscles. These stop the respiratory muscles working and allow the surgeon to get at the chest. Breathing must be kept going during the operation by a life-support machine. The patient's nose and mouth are connected to a machine filled with oxygen and other gases, and a bellows-mechanism forces the gases into the lungs.

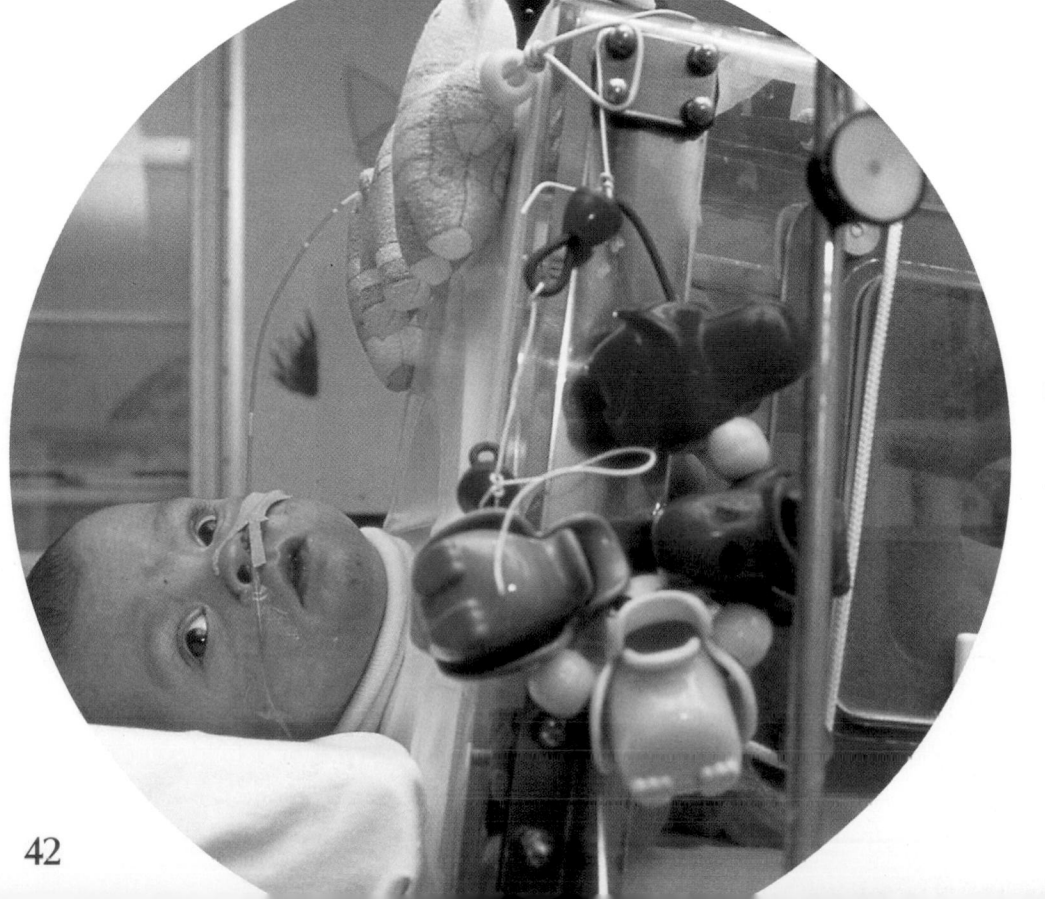

**Intensive care**
This patient in an intensive care unit in hospital is attached to a ventilator to assist breathing.

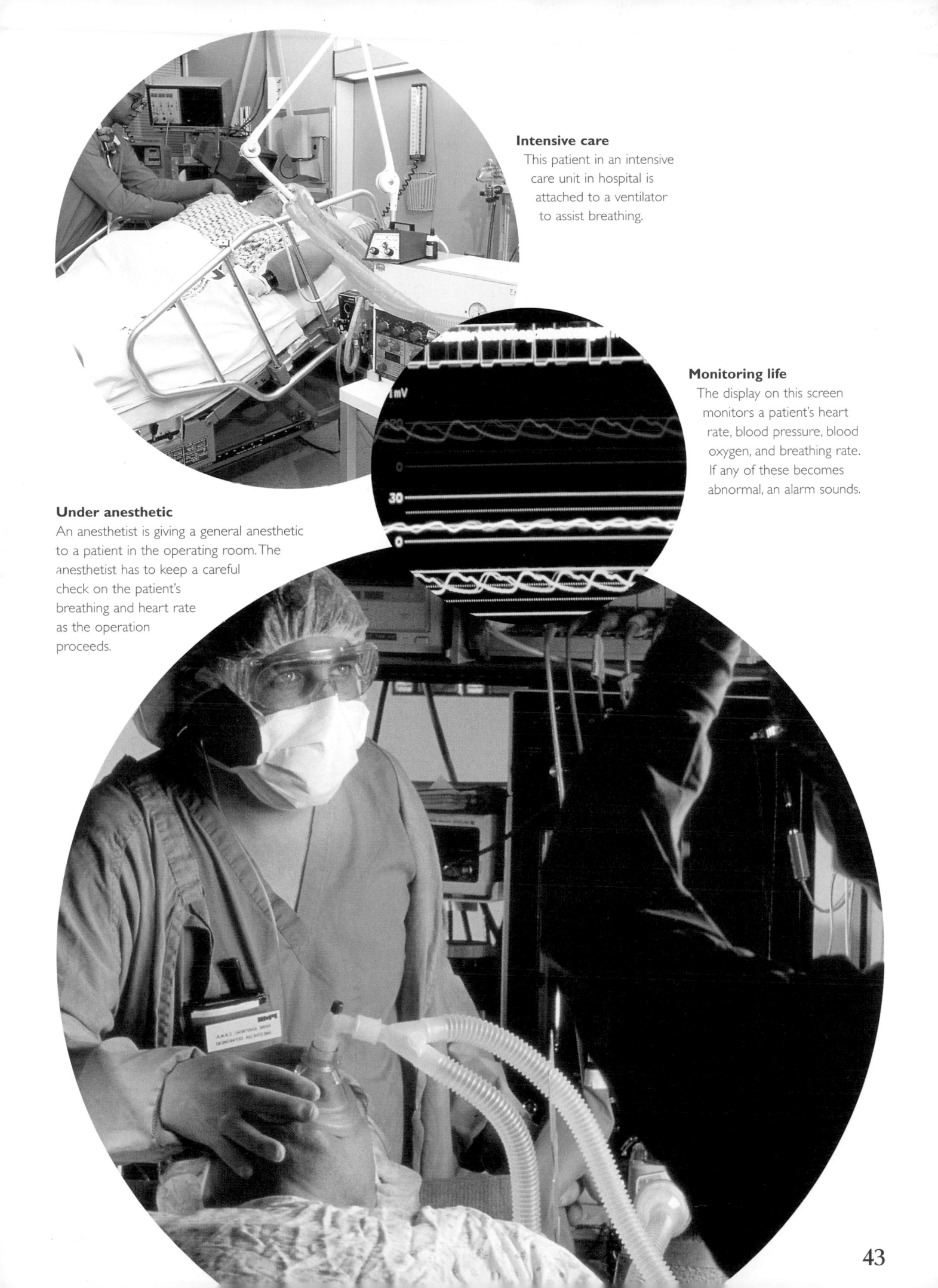

### Intensive care
This patient in an intensive care unit in hospital is attached to a ventilator to assist breathing.

### Monitoring life
The display on this screen monitors a patient's heart rate, blood pressure, blood oxygen, and breathing rate. If any of these becomes abnormal, an alarm sounds.

### Under anesthetic
An anesthetist is giving a general anesthetic to a patient in the operating room. The anesthetist has to keep a careful check on the patient's breathing and heart rate as the operation proceeds.

43

# EMERGENCIES & FIRST AID

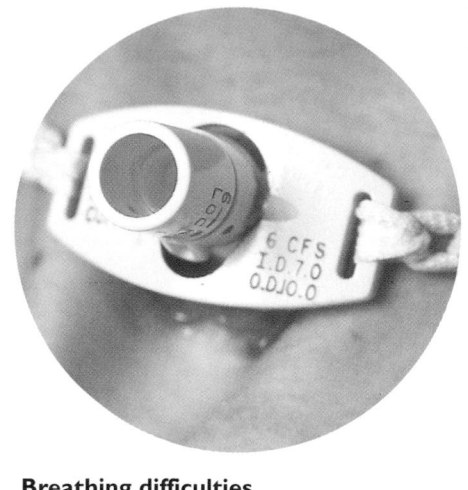

**Breathing difficulties**
Because of breathing difficulties, this person has undergone an operation called a tracheostomy. An opening is made into the windpipe, and a tube, called a tracheostomy tube, is inserted into it. Air is then pumped into the lungs through the tube.

If someone is deprived of oxygen for more than four minutes, they suffer brain damage. Death follows if breathing is not started again quickly. So in any emergency that causes a person to stop breathing, it is essential to get the respiratory system working again as soon as possible.

Severe blows to the head, suffocation, heart attacks, and electric shock can all cause breathing to stop. If the lungs are undamaged, mouth-to-mouth resuscitation – breathing directly into the patient's airways – can get breathing going again. Then heart massage may be needed to restart the heart if it has stopped beating.

Choking on an object that is blocking the airways can also stop breathing and be extremely dangerous. A piece of food "going down the wrong way" can actually cause someone to choke to death. In 1974 an American doctor called Henry Heimlich developed a technique for clearing such blockages. Known as the Heimlich maneuver, it involves making powerful thrusts to the sufferer's abdomen to force a rush of air up through the airways and clear the obstruction.

Such techniques need to be done correctly if they are to succeed and are best learned in a simple first aid course. Do not try them yourself without proper training.

**Breathing too fast**
Sometimes, perhaps because they are feeling anxious, a person may breathe too quickly and deeply. This is called hyperventilation, and it makes the person even more anxious. Breathing into a paper bag for a short time can be helpful.

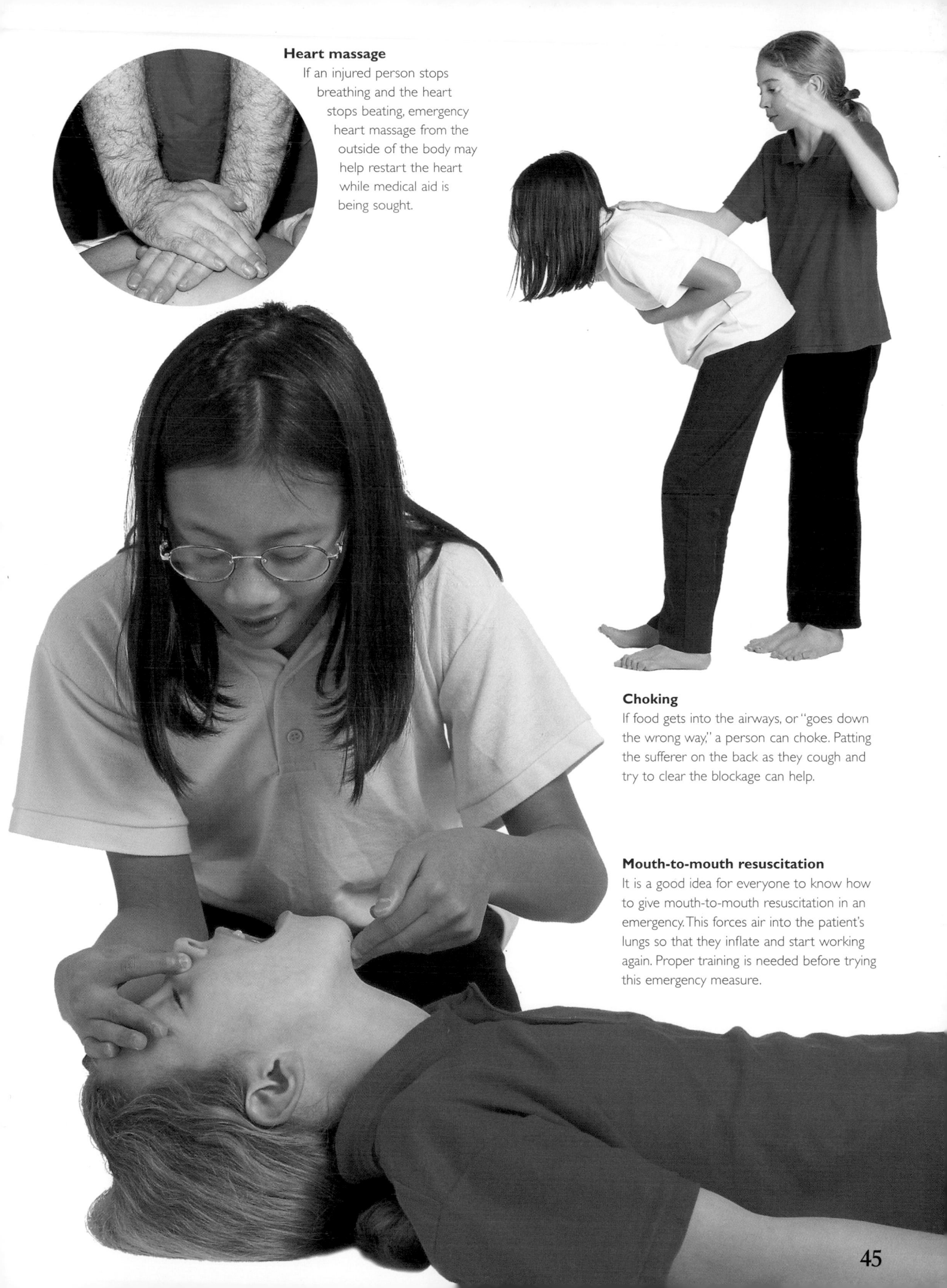

### Heart massage

If an injured person stops breathing and the heart stops beating, emergency heart massage from the outside of the body may help restart the heart while medical aid is being sought.

### Choking

If food gets into the airways, or "goes down the wrong way," a person can choke. Patting the sufferer on the back as they cough and try to clear the blockage can help.

### Mouth-to-mouth resuscitation

It is a good idea for everyone to know how to give mouth-to-mouth resuscitation in an emergency. This forces air into the patient's lungs so that they inflate and start working again. Proper training is needed before trying this emergency measure.

# GLOSSARY

**ALLERGY** (Al-lur-jee)
A sensitivity to a particular substance. Pollen is one of the substances that can irritate the respiratory system. It can trigger the allergic reaction called hay fever, which causes sneezing and running nose and eyes.

**ALVEOLUS** (Al-vee-o-luss)
One of the many tiny air spaces in the lungs where oxygen passes into the blood and carbon dioxide passes out of it.

**ANESTHESIA** (An-us-theez-yuh)
A process by which a patient about to have an operation is given gases that make him or her lose consciousness and feel no pain.

**ARTERY**
One of the blood vessels that takes blood from the heart to other parts of the body.

**ASTHMA** (Az-muh)
A disease of the lungs in which the airways become narrowed and breathing is difficult. Sufferers usually make a wheezing noise as they breathe.

**BRONCHIAL TREE** (Bron-kee-ull)
Network of branching tubes inside the lungs.

**BRONCHIOLE** (Bron-kee-ole)
One of the many branches of a bronchus and the smallest of the airways in the bronchial tree.

**BRONCHUS** (Bron-kuss)
One of the two tubes into which the trachea, or windpipe, divides. Each bronchus branches again into smaller and smaller airways.

**CAPILLARIES** (Ka-pill-uh-reez)
Thin-walled blood vessels that surround each alveolus. Oxygen passes from the alveolus through the thin walls of the capillary and into the blood.

**CARBON DIOXIDE**
A gas produced by the body's cells as they break down nutrients and supply energy. Carbon dioxide must be removed from the body. It is carried in the blood to the lungs and breathed out. Carbon dioxide is used by plants in the process of photosynthesis.

**CARTILAGE** (Kar-till-ij)
A tough bendy material that makes up the end of the nose, much of the external ears, and covers the ends of bones where they meet at joints.

**CILIA** (Sill-ee-uh)
Tiny hairlike structures that line the inside of the airways. Cilia beat to move mucus and dust and other particles upward and out of the airways.

**DIAPHRAGM** (Die-uh-fram)
The sheet of muscle that separates the chest from the abdomen. When you breathe in, the diaphragm flattens, making the chest cavity bigger. When you breathe out, the diaphragm goes back to its normal position.

**EPIGLOTTIS** (Eppy-glott-iss)
A small flap of tissue at the top of the larynx. This flap covers the airway when we swallow food or drink and stops it going down the wrong way.

**HEMOGLOBIN** (Hee-mow-glow-bin)
The red pigment in red blood cells. Oxygen combines with hemoglobin in the blood and is then carried to all parts of the body.

**INTERCOSTAL MUSCLES**
Muscles attached to the ribs. Before we breathe in, these muscles contract and move the ribs outward, increasing the size of the chest cavity.

**LARYNX** (La-rinks)
A structure made of cartilage positioned in the front of the throat at the top of the trachea. Air passes through the larynx on its way to the lungs. Also called the voice box, the larynx contains the vocal cords. These vibrate when air passes through them and produce sound.

**LUNG**
One of the two large spongy organs that fill most of the chest. The lungs are filled with the many-branched tubes of the bronchial tree through which air passes.

**MITOCHONDRION**
(Mite-uh-kon-dree-un)
A structure in a cell that uses oxygen to convert sugars such as glucose into energy.

**MUCUS** (Mew-kuss)
A sticky fluid made by cells in the mucous membrane, which lines the airways. It traps most of the particles that enter the upper airways and prevents them reaching the lungs.

**OXYGEN**
A gas that is present in the air around us. The body's cells need oxygen in order to grow and to break down nutrients and supply the body with energy. Without oxygen cells die.

**PHARYNX** (Fa-rinks)
The throat cavity through which air travels on its way to the lungs.

**PULMONARY ARTERY** (Pull-mun-er-ee)
One of the blood vessels that carries blood from the heart to the lungs.

**PULMONARY VEIN**
One of the blood vessels that carries oxygenated blood from the lungs to the heart to be pumped around the body.

**RESPIRATION**
The process by which the body's cells use oxygen in order to break down nutrients and supply the body with energy.

**RIBS**
The twelve pairs of bones that curve around from the backbone to the chest. Together they form a bony cage that protects the heart and lungs.

**TRACHEA** (Trayck-ee-uh)
A short tube that joins the upper part of the respiratory system to the bronchi, which lead into the lungs. It is also called the windpipe.

**VOCAL CORDS**
Two pieces of membrane inside the larynx. When we breathe normally, air passes through a wide gap between the cords. When we speak, muscles close the gap between the cords. As air squeezes through the gap, the cords vibrate, making sounds.

# SET INDEX

# Acknowledgments

The publishers wish to thank the following for supplying photographs for this book: Biophoto Associates/Science Photo Library (SPL) 18 (TL); Martin Bond/SPL 35; Dr. Tony Brain/SPL front cover (C), 6 (TL), 19 (TR); BSIP VEM/SPL 2 (C), 12 (B), 39 (TL); Van Bucher/SPL 42 (TL); Oscar Burriel/SPL 40 (TL); Dr. Jeremy Burgess/SPL 41 (B); CDC/SPL 39 (TR); Dr. Ray Clark and Dr. Mervyn Goff/SPL 6 (CL); CNRI/SPL 3 (CR, BL), 4 (C), 7, 10 (B), 11 (CL), 13 (TR, BL), 16 (BL), 17 (BL), 31 (BR), 32 (CL); Dyson Appliances Ltd. 16 (CL); Prof. C. Ferlaud/CNRI/SPL 14 (CL, BL); James Holmes/Reed Nurse/SPL, 8 (BL); Institut Pasteur/CNRI/SPL 40 (CL); Camilla Jessel/Cystic Fibrosis Trust 38 (CL); James King-Holmes/SPL 43 (C); Bill Longcore/SPL 8 (CR); Damien Lovegrove/SPL, 24 (B); Will McIntyre/SPL, 26 (TL); Will and Deni McIntyre/SPL 43 (B); Matt Meadows/Peter Arnold Inc./SPL 37 (TL, BR); Astrid and Hanns-Frieder Michler/SPL back cover (CL), 12 (TL), 19 (BL), 38 (TL); Miles Kelly Archives 30 (TR), 31 (TR), 32 (TL), 33 (TL, TR), 34 (BR); Hank Morgan /SPL 43 (TL); Prof. P. Motta/Dept. of Anatomy/University "La Sapienza," Rome/SPL front cover (BL), 23 (CR, BL), 29 (T); Profs. P. Motta and S. Nottola/Dept. of Anatomy/University "La Sapienza," Rome/SPL 6 (B), 17 (TL); Profs. P. Motta, Correr, and S. Nottola/University "La Sapienza," Rome/SPL 6 (B); National Medical Slide Bank 44 (TL, BL), 45 (TL); Panos Pictures 32 (BR); Alfred Pasieka/SPL 11 (TR); Petit Format/Nestle/SPL 24 (TL), 25 (C); D. Phillips/SPL front cover (BR), 22 (B); Rex Features London 15 (B), 26 (C), 33 (C), 36 (TR); David Scharf/SPL 41 (TR); SPL 16 (TL), 39 (B); Dr. Gary Settles/SPL 38 (BR); Pat Spillane 10 (TL, model Chloe Boulton), 15 (TL, C, TR, model Africa Green), 21 (model Africa Green), 27 (model Darren Richardson-Jackson), 28 (TR, BL, model Puspita McKenzie), 29 (B, model Puspita McKenzie), 45 (TR, B, models Chloe Boulton, Puspita McKenzie); Jim Stevenson/SPL 34 (CL, BL), 37 (CR); The Stock Market 26 (BR), 30 (B), 31; Penny Tweedie/SPL 42 (BL); Hattie Young /SPL 34 (TL).